The B2B S

A Hands-On Guide to Generating More Leads, Closing More Deals, and Working Less

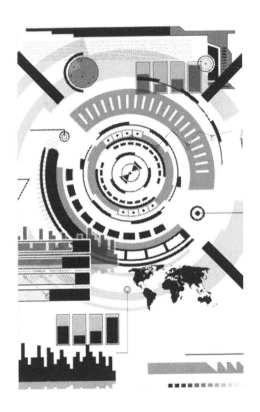

By Dan Englander
SalesSchema.com

Table of Contents

Resources: Do This First!

This is an analog and e-reader text, but the strategies have major online components. This book contains "**Action Items**"—or assignments to complete as you progress. Also, you'll get spreadsheets, text documents, and other downloadables.

Go here to get all the Resources:
http://www.salesschema.com/b2b-book-enroll/

B2B Sales Resources

Note: Click "File" > "Make a copy" to input your own data

Chapter 1

Lead Generation Goals Spreadsheet

https://docs.google.com/spreadsheets/d/1s76xBERRFYVtv86iQiT2_Z-3cBDnSj4EbYFzXwnmYwQ/edit?usp=sharing

For the sake of efficiency, I encourage you to have these resources on hand before proceeding because I'll be referencing them frequently.

To get these materials, I'm going to ask for your email address because I want to ensure you exclusive access. More importantly, you'll also get a newsletter, which is the best way for me to keep you informed about new strategies and tools.

Getting Started

As salespeople, we have our faults, but you can't accuse us of lacking self-awareness. After all, progress, success, stagnation, and failure is spelled out, clear as day, by the numbers we hit or miss. As such, you probably know a thing or two about your sales game. Maybe this knowledge is top of mind, or it might need prying out with a bit of self-assessment. And because you chose to read a book that promises sales growth, it's likely that you're already convinced that improvement is possible. That said, the most common challenges tend to loom large on our psyches, and they recur.

Maybe you struggle each quarter to generate enough leads, or you might not know what "enough" should really mean. Maybe you feel like you waste time trying to engage with people who will never buy from you. Maybe you feel like your sales conversations lack a clear direction, or that you're at a loss for the right words. Or perhaps you feel like you're generally stuck in a rut.

This book is for salespeople of all stripes: entrepreneurs, business development professionals, business owners, and anyone who comes into direct contact with leads, prospects and customers. We'll deal with hurdles like the ones above, and you'll improve with the help of modern technology and a small library of scripts and templates, designed to keep your conversations planned and goal-focused.

Who am I?

Like many people, I once assumed that sales was the realm of slick-talking, hard-charging, naturally-persuasive types. Though not an introvert, I knew this wasn't me, so I stayed away. After moving through different marketing-related positions, I was hired as the first employee and Senior Account Manager at IdeaRocket, a business animation shop based in New York. Considering the company started as two people, the founder and me, I wore a lot of hats, and my most important duty was sales and business development. The pressure was on to close deals or close our doors.

I wish I could say I immediately rose to the occasion, but I floundered for quite a while. My sales process went something like this: I'd get an inbound lead (i.e., the customer would see an ad and contact us), or I'd write a cold email. If I was lucky, that outreach would lead to a phone call where I'd discuss the product, features, benefits, and so on. I'd send them a quote, then I'd wait. More often than not, I'd never hear from them again. It was a losing process, but it worked out OK—for a while.

Before long, my sales began to drop off. After a few really bad months I decided I had to do something. I needed to take action to educate myself on *how to sell* more effectively. So I started searching. I talked to lots of people. I underwent traditional coaching, as well as self-driven research into new technologies and approaches. I got insight from my successful peers.

From this experience, I made two observations that disrupt the traditional view of a successful salesperson.

My first observation: Genuine curiosity, about your prospect and his or her business, is powerful. It builds the understanding needed to be trustworthy and persuasive. With that in mind, sales doesn't have to be the realm of manipulators or verbal svengalis. You can achieve equal, if not greater, success by becoming a great listener. This means opening your ears and asking the right questions before suggesting this or that solution. Your reserved friend who listens to you complain about a rough day at work, and asks you to elaborate, is perhaps more poised to close deals than your gregarious socialite buddy.

My second observation: The sales process starts long before you speak to your prospect. This is more true than ever as marketing and sales meld together with the help of new technology and readily available information. Salespeople are no longer the wardens of privileged data and details. As such, the role now involves developing and curating information, while combating misconceptions. It means getting analytical and understanding your prospect's journey before picking up the phone. Apps, tools, and high-tech shortcuts make this possible, and you'll learn all about these assets later. Furthermore, new tech resources allow you to multiply your results by leveraging a team, which might include outsourced lead generation specialists, for example.

My investment of time and energy in gaining this new understanding transformed my results. I won more deals and turned things around; IdeaRocket tripled sales in a year's time. By the time I left IdeaRocket in 2014, our revenue was above seven figures. We had 16 Fortune 500s in our client roster. We grew to a team of eight full-time employees and 10-15 freelancers, and we moved into a large studio space in Midtown Manhattan.

Today I run Sales Schema, a company devoted to helping organizations with sales, account management, and digital marketing.

Goals

Before we go much further, I'd like you to think about your present sales situation. Think about the aspects you consider strong, and others you consider weak; basically, I want you to envision where you stand today.

Next, think about where you want to be in the near future, after completing this book, and honing your craft. Maybe this exercise is straightforward: perhaps you have a quota set for you by your company, or you otherwise have firm targets in place. If so, kudos! On the other hand, it's possible you don't have a goal set; maybe you're not in a high-pressure scenario where you "need" to improve, per se, but you just want to get a leg up on your competition. Regardless, *I* have a goal. Perhaps it's a little aspirational, or god forbid, *sales-y*, but it's my goal nonetheless.

I hope to triple your sales within one year.

Remember: I used these same strategies to triple *my* revenue, and I think you can too if you commit yourself fully. That said, you can probably appreciate that without knowing your particular industry, business landscape, customer demographic, and a plethora of other factors, it's very difficult for me to *guarantee* you the these results.

But this is what I will guarantee you:

Leveraging the strategies in this book *will* equip you to close more deals and drive more revenue. However, you must apply everything you learn. You must complete all of the "Action Items" that accompany the lessons. You must get off and running with the tools I offer.

Note for Readers of Mastering Account Management

I am grateful to those who have read and enjoyed my other books. For *Mastering Account Management* readers, please be aware that this book includes some material that was originally presented there. However, it's updated and expanded within the framework of the entire B2B sales process, and I'm confident that you'll get a fresh experience.

Summary of Chapters

You'll transform your sales process in five chapters:

Chapter 1 presents the first step in the process: your daily and continuous **Lead Generation** effort. First, you will determine your daily lead generation goal, then you will develop your process, systematize it and then outsource it, allowing someone else to generate leads for you while you pursue more important tasks.

Chapter 2 focuses on the **First Conversation**. This is your chance to qualify your prospect, ask revealing questions, learn about the buying situation, and pitch your product in a persuasive way. To help you craft your own ideas, you'll look to the *Conversation Blueprint*.

Chapter 3 picks up where the first sales conversation ends, focusing on **Following Up and Closing the Sale**. This step tackles setting up future conversations and guiding the prospect through the process until a decision is made: "yes" or "no," but never "maybe."

Chapter 4 highlights general **Skills** you should build into your repertoire. You'll develop them by rehearsing and revising your script, challenging yourself, defeating doubt and fear of rejection, and taking the right steps to drive referrals. Also, there's a quick "life hack" I think you'll enjoy.

Finally, **Chapter 5** demonstrates a few very useful **Apps, Tools, and High-Tech Shortcuts** to make you better, faster, and stronger. With these tools you can gain a competitive advantage, add urgency to slow-moving prospects, automate pre-meeting research, and follow up at the most relevant time.

This book concludes with a valuable list of online resources. By the time you're done, you will have the tools you need to succeed. And it all begins on the next page.

Reminder: Don't forget to grab the Resources before getting started!

Ready? Let's begin!

before we go much further.
I'd like you to envision where you stand today and where you want your business to go.

1. The Lead Generation Blueprint

Resources needed:
- *Lead Gen Goals Worksheet*
- *Target List Blueprint*
- *Email Permutator*
- *Cold Email Template*
- *Lead Gen Freelancer Blueprint*
- *Job Post Template*

Objective: Multiply your efforts, build a steady stream of prospects and enjoy new free time by systematizing and outsourcing lead generation.

If you're not lucky enough to be in a position where your marketing brings leads *to* you, then you will need to find them yourself through prospecting, or lead generation.

The process of lead generation, as I will present it here, consists of the following steps:

Set a Goal — You will set your monthly sales goal, and use it to determine the number of cold leads you should reach out to each day.

Master — You will set up and master the lead generation process, finding the right people and reaching out to them in a persuasive way.

Systematize and Outsource — You will prepare a step-by-step process, enabling a virtual assistant to carry out lead generation for you.

Tracking down new leads is a numbers game, and it ties directly into your overall success. The more people you can get yourself in front of, the greater your likelihood of landing appointments, and ultimately making a sale. My methods lean heavily on technology combined with outsourced help, so you can multiply your efforts and rack up as many leads as you can handle. The technology, which ties to email and other mediums, will let you familiarize prospects with your offering, and warm up your cold leads before reaching out by phone or in person.

Does this daily lead generation mission sound a bit intimidating? If so, don't worry; it overwhelmed me at one time too. This chapter is all about making the process approachable and winnable. It is a huge task, but giant, scary tasks never seem as bad when you cut them down to size. Soon you'll do that by setting the right lead generation goals for your business. You'll figure out what you (and eventually your outsourced help) will need to do each day in order to produce future sales.

Lead Generation: Set a Goal

First, we will figure out how many potential buyers you need to contact on a daily basis, in order to produce a certain amount of monthly earnings. But before we do, let's define a few things you will need to know before filling out the *Lead Generation Goals Spreadsheet*:

Lead Generation Goals Spreadsheet

File Edit View Insert Format Data Tools Add-ons Help   Last edit was on April 22

	A	B
1		
2	Directions:	
3	To input your own data, Click "File" --> "Make a Copy"	
4	STEP 1: Input your monthly Sales Goal	
5	STEP 2: Input your Average Deal Size	
6	STEP 3: Input your target Conversion Rate	
7	STEP 4: Input your target Close Rate	
8		
9		
10		
11		
12		
13	Sales Goal (monthly)	$50,000.00
14	Average Deal Size	$17,500.00
15	Deals (monthly)	5
16	Conversion Rate	3.00%
17	Close Rate	10.00%
18	Prospects in Pipeline (monthly)	48
19	Cold Leads (monthly)	1534
20	Working days (monthly)	22
21	**I need to contact this many Cold Leads each day...**	76

Sales Goal (monthly) — This is self-explanatory: Simply, this is your desired total monthly sales.

Average Deal Size — When you win a deal, what is the average dollar value of that deal? If you don't know this off the top of your head, you can estimate it for now; you'll calibrate things as you go along.

Target Close Rate — This is the percentage of qualified prospects you would expect to win business with, after you've landed an appointment with them.   ("Qualified prospects" are people who have a budget and a schedule for getting started, who are relatively interested in your offer [or one of your competitors].)   Think of it this way: If you were granted meetings with 100 people, all of whom have budgets, are considering your offering (or a competitor's), and will be ready to get started soon, how many of these people would you expect to close? Again, rough estimates are fine for now.   (That number of people is your percentage.)

Target Conversion Rate — This is the percentage of cold leads you expect to move into your pipeline each month. If you're unfamiliar, you can think of your "pipeline" as your main sales dashboard that shows who you're in the trenches with — the people you're conversing with, qualifying, and working to close. If you're having trouble, this might help: Imagine that, over the course of a month, a team of lead generation experts reaches out to 10,000 qualified potential buyers, trying to win you appointments. The targets are diverse, equally spread out among your buyer groups. How many of the 10,000 people would you expect to agree to having a meeting with you? (Divide that number by 100 to get a percentage.)

The Lead Gen Goals Spreadsheet is a calculator, which will determine how many cold leads you need to reach out to each day. You will see there are cells within the spreadsheet where you input the four values you determined above. But there is one more cell you may wish to consider: "Working days (monthly)". Populate this field based on how many days you plan on working in a month. To give you a frame of reference, the average month consists of about 22 weekdays.

* * *

Example:
- Sales goal (monthly): $80,000
- Average Deal Size: $17,500
- Target Close Rate: 10%
- Target Conversion Rate: 3%
- Working Days (monthly): 20

14

I need to contact this many cold leads each day: 76

* * *

In this example, 76 cold leads must be contacted each day in order to meet the monthly sales goal. That might seem like a huge number—and it is—but don't worry. Soon you will learn a super-simple and effective research process for cold outreach. Also, before long you will be multiplying your efforts by outsourcing lead generation.

AeroLeads Lead Generation ROI Calculator

The above method should work well for many, if not most, situations. But if your sales process is considerably more complex or lengthy, the following tool will help you forecast ROI and set accurate goals. Provided by AeroLeads, a lead generation research company, the _Lead Generation ROI Calculator_ is powerful (reminder: analog readers can find this and all future links in _External Resources_, at the end of the book). For demonstration purposes, the tool starts with sample numbers. A particularly cool feature is its differentiation between inbound and outbound leads. **Inbound** refers to leads that "come to you"; advertising is a common means of generating these. **Outbound** refers to leads that a salesperson has to actively seek out.

Let's define the tool's parameters:

Monthly Revenue Goal — Same as "Sales Goal (monthly)" from the earlier method.

Average Sales Price — Same as "Average Deal Size" above.

Percentage Revenue — Percent of revenue that comes from inbound and outbound leads.

Visit to Lead Rate — Can be thought of as "marketing qualified leads", or MQLs. This is the rate at which people who are exposed to your product (often via ads or cold outreach) have shown interest.

Lead to Opportunity Rate — Can be translated to "sales qualified leads", or SQLs. This is the rate at which you discover that people who express interest are serious: usually they have a budget, a need for your product, and somewhat of a timeline.

Opportunity Win Rate — Same as "Close Rate".

Average Cost Per Lead — This is sometimes difficult to determine, but basically it's your close rate (i.e., your Opportunity Win Rate) multiplied by your gross profit per sale. Your gross profit, in this case, is your average deal size minus the direct cost of providing the product or services. (Note: This cost should include the cost of acquisition, including sales-related expenses like advertising; it should not include fixed costs like utility bills or custodial services.)

After you click the "Calculate" button, you will see the number of people you should shoot for in terms of visits, leads, opportunities and wins. The results will help you develop a budget and return on investment (ROI) for your inbound and outbound campaigns.

The truth is, the longer you've been doing business, the more data you will have, and the easier this information will be to determine. If you are a new business, this process will involve some guesswork. Regardless, it's never too early to start planning around these metrics.

Lead Generation: Master

Although lead generation *is* a numbers game, you can still get really targeted. But you'll need to stay organized. Eventually you should adopt a customer relationship management system, or CRM, if you haven't already. Selecting a CRM is outside the scope of this book, but a few great options are Close.io, PipelineDeals, and the Hubspot Sales Platform.

For our purposes at the moment, you can use a Google Spreadsheet for your target list and prospect profiles. This option is convenient because it's simple and easily sharable. A good model of this is the *Target List Blueprint*.

Name	Title	Company	Email	LinkedIn URL	Twitter URL	Phone	Dates Contacted	Notes

(handwritten across table: What's my Ideal Client Like?)

To start building a high-quality target list, creating prospect profiles is a valuable exercise. This will help you identify what types of people you are going after, as well as their tendencies and priorities. In fact, you should keep your prospect profiles wherever you keep your target list. If it's in your CRM, store your profiles there. It's okay to focus on those who will bring you in the door; you don't have to find the decision-maker right away.

Example:

Buyer Group:	IT Executives
Titles:	CTO, Head of Development, VP of Technology
Gender Breakdown:	M: 80% / F: 20%
Examples:	Joe Smith, Head of Development at XYZ Tech.; Kamal Khan, CTO at Mastertech
Fictional Profile:	Bob is the CTO and co-founder of his startup IT Firm, ACME Technologies. He's in his mid thirties, and he's married with young children. His favorite sites for staying up to date on his industry are "Around the Storage Block" and GigaOM. Bob draws $80,000/year from the company, but he looks to double that number within the next three years. He speaks our language, and not much explanation when describing our product. He cares about our track record and our differentiators.

When you create prospect profiles and conduct research, be sure to focus on one buyer group at a time because it will be easier to conceptualize a specific messaging and outreach strategy for each group.

To create your profiles, fill out the following:

Buyer Group — Name your buyer group: "big ad agencies" for example.

Titles — Enter a few common job titles for the people you're pursuing, like "Creative Director" or "Creative Lead".

Gender Breakdown — Enter an approximate gender breakdown for this group.

Examples — Enter examples of real people you're worked with that fit the profile, like "Bob Faucet, ACME Plumbers".

Fictional Profile — Get your creative juices flowing, and write a fictional description of a typical member. This exercise will help you understand your ideal buyers in a more personal way. Who is this person? What is their background? What websites or publications do they read? What is their experience with your product or industry? What is their general perception of your product or industry?

Building Your Target List with LinkedIn

When it comes to building your list, LinkedIn is a great place to start. Best of all, it's free! You do not need a paid premium account.

Your goal here is to find the number of contacts you came up with earlier, using the *Lead Gen Goals Worksheet*. Again, this is the number of cold leads you must contact each day in order to hit your monthly sales goal. But you can't add just anyone to your list; you have to be targeted in your pursuit of high-quality leads.

Step 1: Build Your Advanced Search

First, log in to LinkedIn. From your main page, click the "Advanced" link at the top, to the right of the search bar. This will bring you to the "Advanced People Search" page.

Here's the approach you'll take: Start by going for a wide net, and filter it down to the cream of the crop. These high-value leads will enter your target list.

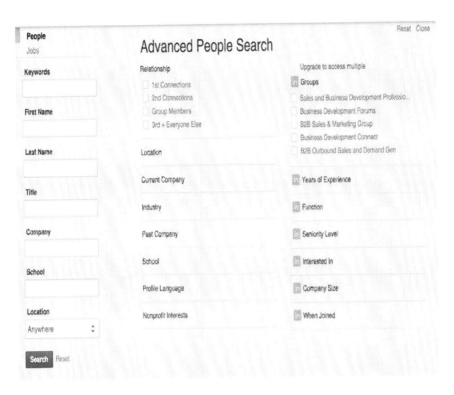

Input the following into each noted "Advanced Search" parameter:

Title — Enter those you determined earlier from your prospect profiles. Here you can use boolean phrases: For example, you can search for "CMO OR VP of Marketing". For a quick crash course in boolean search terms, check out this short guide from UC Berkeley titled "Basic Search Tips and Advanced Boolean Explained".

Current Company — Plug in as many relevant companies as you can. Remember, you're going for a wide net of results. If you do not yet have company targets in mind, try this method:

Open a new window and bring up LinkedIn profiles for a few of your previous customers' companies. On those company pages, scroll down and look on the right-hand margin of the page for a section titled "People Also Viewed". This will tell you about similar companies, which are often good targets.

You can do the same for your competitors' customers. Scan on a competitor's website or LinkedIn page to determine the organizations they've worked with.

Once you have a solid list of companies, plug them into the "Current Company" field. The number will depend on your situation, but you should aim to generate as many results as possible for the first run-through.

Step 2: Filter Results

After populating the search fields with titles and companies, click the "Search" button. You should have a robust list of people from which to choose. Scan through a couple pages just to make sure your results are generally relevant.

Now you'll start filtering. From your search results, open profiles for three to five people who appear particularly relevant. Start recording their details in your target list, including their names, titles, and companies. Don't worry about email addresses yet; we'll find those soon. But be sure to include their LinkedIn URLs for future reference.

Now that you have a few ideal targets, scan through their profiles and look for certain keywords and jargon that relates to your offering, like "IT vendor" or "acquisition" for example. Bring these recurring terms into the **Keywords** parameter in the advanced search above, and populate new results. This will let you filter your wide net of data down to high-value targets.

Take a second to copy these terms into your target list so that all the important details on each buyer group are in one place.

Also, it's often helpful to get inspiration for industry jargon by scanning the profiles of your previous customers; this adds a level of validation to your research.

Continue filtering with keywords to narrow your results, and add target companies to expand them. Keep doing this process until you have the desired number of high-quality targets; you can bang out a few days worth of leads, according to your quota from earlier, in one session if you'd like.

This process might seem time-consuming, but don't worry: you'll get outsourced help before long.

Find Any Email Address

Why email, and not LinkedIn messages or other channels? Because most people check their inboxes multiple times per day. This is where you want to be.

As we've covered, lead generation is a numbers game. The trick is finding the right balance between quantity and quality. When it comes to researching addresses, we're pursuing the former. For efficiency's sake, Rule #1 of email research is this: Don't waste too much time on any one address. Skip problem targets as needed, and circle back later if you want.

To determine your email research approach, ask yourself this: Is your target in a large or small company?

Small Company Email Research: Rapportive

Rapportive (Rapportive.com) is a GMail app that works with either Google Chrome or Firefox web browsers, so you'll need one of those to get started. Don't worry: You won't have to actually send messages from GMail if you'd rather not.

Once you have Rapportive set up in GMail, open up the *Email Permutator Spreadsheet*.

Step 1: Develop Common Email Permutations

Fill in information about your target in the spreadsheet, including first, middle and last names, as well as the address's domain. (This is everything that would follow the at sign [@] in the address. For example, "idearocketanimation.com".) Make sure the information you put in does not include any spaces because spaces will show up in the results. Once you're done, the right side of the spreadsheet will list permutations. For example,"dan.englander@idearocketanimation.com", "dan@idearocketanimation.com", "denglander@idearocketanimation.com", and so on.

Step 2: Determine Correct Email Address With GMail + Rapportive

Compose a new message in GMail. Copy and paste the top five most likely permutations into the "To" line of the message, then scroll over each one. Continue the above process until a picture and/or a social icon appears in Rapportive, which means the address is correct.

This method is suitable for small companies because, in my experience, employees are more likely to link their company addresses to social networks. If an email is not linked to a social account, it won't appear in Rapportive.

Large Company Email Research: Finding Email Conventions

Most large companies have a fixed email convention they use for most, if not all, of their employees. Although there are exceptions, once you learn this convention, you can contact almost anyone as long as you know their full name.

Finding large company addresses consists of two major steps:

1. **Determine the email address convention**
2. **Test out and verify your target's address**

For step 1, let's start where most searches begin: Google. We're going to use Google search modifiers to find exactly what we're looking for. For more on modifiers, check out the articles linked in the External Resources section, at the end of the book.

To put modifiers into action, let's try to find the email convention for a large company: How about IBM?

First, we want to find a web page that might have an IBM email address on it. We would try something like this:

```
site:ibm.com + "email" OR "contact us"
```

This request searches for ONLY results located at ibm.com, that contain either the word "email" or the phrase "contact us".

With the help of modifiers, you would find that IBM offers a remarkable gift for finding employee addresses. Try this search:

```
site:ibm.com + "employee directory"
```

The top result is IBM's employee directory, where you provide the first and last name of your target, and IBM will spit out the employee's email address and phone number. It's likely that other companies have employee directories, which will save you tons of research time. If you find a directory, do yourself a favor and bookmark it.

If you aren't so lucky, review a few pages of search results. On any web page, you can use the keyboard shortcut Ctrl+F (Command+F on Mac) to bring up a search bar, and enter the address's domain (Example: "@ibm.com"), or something similar.

Searching by Press Release

Another great strategy is looking for the company's press releases, because often there is a PR person with a correct email convention attached to the public statement. Try this search:

```
site:ibm.com + "press release" OR "PR" OR
"@ibm.com"
```

Notice I have included the email address's domain ("@ibm.com"). This is especially useful because if you find the at sign (@) followed by the domain, it's usually an email address.

Keep in mind that some companies have subsidiary domains, such as "us.ibm.com". Often, these addresses are used for international employees.

If you decide to dig deeper into press releases, you should also check out PR Newswire (prnewswire.com), a major press release hub. Search for the company and see what comes up. In our example, we'd search for the domain "ibm.com", check a few pages in the results and use Ctrl+F (or Command+F) to hunt for the convention.

More Helpful Research Tools

If you find you are having difficulty, there are a couple of online services that may help you. First, there is an Email Lookup service available from Intelius (Intelius.com). The downside is that it's not free; it's $5 per record, or $2 if you also buy a membership.

When you think you have cracked the company's email convention, you can use a tool like the Free Email Verifier at verify-email.org. Enter the expected email address of your target and see if it reports as valid. If it does, then your search is likely over. Do the same for your other targets from the same company, but remember that this website only allows you to search 10 times per hour; any more than that and they'll ask you to pay.

Finally, there is an online tool called Norbert (VoilaNorbert.com), which will give you a few free email searches. Their price structure is for unlimited usage: $5 per hour, $10 per day, and $50 per month; or you can buy searches by volume at $0.25 per search. If you have a bunch of names in a comma separated (CSV) spreadsheet, you can upload it for speedy results.

If Nothing Else Works . . .

If these strategies aren't working, and if you have time—remember, don't spend more than a few minutes on any one address—there are a few things you can try. First, you can search for your target's personal email address. Enter "gmail.com", "yahoo.com", or a few of the common email providers in the permutator, and see what comes up. Then you can use the Rapportive method above. In your email, make sure to mention why you're reaching out on their personal address, and take a soft approach. We'll cover cold emails soon.

If needed, don't be afraid to pick up the phone and call the company, and ask the receptionist (or another gatekeeper) for your target's email address. Be honest: Just tell him or her that you "wanted to get [target's name] some information regarding [your industry or product]." Say that you've had trouble tracking down their address. Worst case, you're denied. No harm done. But more often than not, they will happily help you.

The 13 Components of a Great Cold Email

You've built a list of valuable targets and tracked down their emails. So what are you going to say to these people? Why should they take time out of their busy schedules for you, and potentially open their wallets?

You are about to learn how to craft a persuasive cold outreach email, and later a follow-up strategy. Your message will be much more than the sum of its parts.

The following is a summary of the 13 components of a great cold email. Accompanying this is the *Cold Email Template*, which will underscore the components and give you inspiration when it comes time to craft your own message.

Your primary goal is most likely getting the recipient to commit to a short call or meeting. Whatever your message, keep in mind that you must be able to customize it a bit depending on the recipient.

Each of these components is a tool in your toolbox; you don't necessarily have to use all of them for every undertaking, but leveraging different combinations based on the situation will produce great results.

Cold Email Template:

1. Colloquial Greeting

Hi Rachel,

2. Build familiarity, trust, affection

I recently read the *Inc.* feature on Health365. The way you guys created your user interface is really interesting. In fact, it's been the talk of our developers' break room this week!

3. Connect the comrades   4. Value offering   5. Social proof

Our development team suggested I send you our ROI framework template (attached), given that Meditech.io and ACME Health responded very well. We're rolling it out to two companies this month.

6. Scarcity

7. Straightforward, upfront ask

We specialize is email marketing. I'd like to hear what you're doing in that realm. Even if you don't hire us anytime soon, I promise you will leave with valuable information.

8. Pressure reducer

9. Convenient setup

Can we schedule a quick call on Wednesday @ 2p? We'll need less than 15 minutes.

10. Time reducer

Best,

Dan

Sr. Account Manager, XYZ Company

11. Signature   12. Tracked Link

Subject: "ROI framework template"

13. Keep it simple, casual, familiar.

The 13 components:

1. **Colloquial Greeting** — Email is meant to be conversational. Go with, "Hi [recipient]", not "Dear [Mr. or Ms. recipient]". Over-formality is a direct path to the spam box.

2. **Build Familiarity, Trust, Affection** — Personalize your email, and relate to your recipient by bringing

up one of their past projects or a particular aspect of their company.

3. **Connect the Comrades** — Consider acting as the liaison or introducer. You might lead your pitch with an offer to connect your prospect to like-minded peers in your organization. Owners love speaking with other owners, same goes for developers, producers, lawyers, and other specialists. The promise of a peer, either at the outset or later on, builds comfort.

4. **Value Offering** — Provide something useful. I often recommend offering an "ROI worksheet" for estimating the potential return of your solution. If that's difficult to develop, consider a helpful article that addresses a common problem.

5. **Social Proof** — Make a validation statement, ideally centered on how your product helped companies in your recipient's field.

6. **Scarcity** — Imply that your value offering is privileged information; indicate that your prospect is worthy, and that the material is special.

7. **Note:** The key to the value offering and statements of social proof and scarcity is to be helpful. You are not marketing your product during these steps.

8. **Straightforward, Upfront Ask** — Don't beat around the bush; ask your recipient what you want from them. An ideal goal: Learn about their situation so you can determine if and how your product can help them.

9. **Pressure Reducer** — End by taking the risk out of the potential conversation. Your recipient should know that they will not be forced into a decision.

10. **Convenient Setup** — Offer a clear-cut time for a short call that your recipient can conveniently confirm. This reduces scheduling and mental work.

11. **Time Reducer** — Further reduce the pressure by making it clear that the call will be short; 15 minutes or less is ideal.

12. **Signature** — The conclusion should include your name and title so your prospect knows exactly who you are and what you do.

13. **Tracked Link** — Next to your signature, link to your company's website. If your recipient wants to know about your organization, they can simply click the link. This allows you to tell your story in your most powerful marketing environment, instead of writing a run-on email.

Also, you'll track the link. We'll cover this later, but with a tracked link, you will know that if it's clicked, your message was almost certainly read.

14. **Concise Subject Line** — Keep the subject line of your email simple, casual and familiar. The goal is to get the message opened, and your recipient is most likely to do that if it appears to be a message they would receive from a friend or acquaintance. Stay away from marketing copy.

Action Item #1
Draft your own cold outreach template. Incorporate a few of the 13 elements.

The Stepping Stone Approach
There was a time when email modeled itself on snail mail; the sender would try to deliver all the information in one long message. Not anymore. Today, email is a conversational medium, and has been for a long time.

The above template is aimed at locking down a 15-minute call. You should go for a bigger ask like that when you have a leg up in the situation: Maybe you can provide a major value offering, or you're confident that you can compel a meeting.

Often you can't reach that destination right off the bat, and it's better to ramp up your asks through a stepping stone approach. In these situations, you might start with a thought-provoking question, then send your prospect a useful resource, like a video, case study, or portfolio. After building rapport, you can go for a short meeting.

In each message, pursue no more than one call to action, and put it towards the end so it stands out. Keep the entire message short and mobile-friendly. Make your subject line casual; pretend you're reaching back out to someone you met at a cocktail party.

Check out the below cold email, which resembles an in-person situation: If you met a potential customer at a networking event, you wouldn't rush up to her and immediately demand a meeting. You would start a conversation, have some small talk, and then ask about common challenges.

```
Hi [Prospect],

I'm Dan Englander and I'm Senior Account Manager
at IdeaRocket.  We create animated marketing
videos, which usually live on company homepages.

Since we've worked with a few companies like
yours (Company A & Company B), I'm wondering,
what are you guys doing when it comes to video
marketing?

Best,

Dan

PS: You can check us out here.
```

Here are a few of the most common responses you might receive:

- "We haven't done anything yet in that area."
- "We're working with another provider."
- "We don't have a budget for that."
- "We're too busy."
- "Would you please send me some more information?"

Once you get a response, you're in a conversation, which is exactly where you want to be.

From there, it's time to offer something useful, like a ROI tool, comparison chart, or in-depth article. This is an asset from which your prospect can gain value whether or not they ever hire you.

```
Hi [Prospect],

Thanks for the details [or whatever].  I think
you'll get a lot of use out of the attached ROI
calculator, which will let you measure the
potential impact of a video marketing campaign.
Let me know if any questions come up.

Cheers,

Dan
```

From there, you have a good reason to follow up after a few days to learn about their experience. Call them, or set up a meeting with a message like this:

```
Hi [Prospect],

I wanted to find a time to learn about your
experience with the ROI calculator.  Can we
schedule a 15 min call for Tuesday, 2-3p?

I'd like to see if we can provide the same
results for you.  Even if it turns out we're not
a fit, I promise you'll leave with useful and
helpful information about video marketing.

Best,

Dan
```

To make things easy, be sure to propose a specific time so your prospect can simply confirm or offer an alternative.

Here are a few awesome resources that will help you with cold emails:

First, attach.io features a library of <u>101 Sales Email Templates</u>, which will give you inspiration. Email tracking platforms like <u>Yesware</u> and <u>Sidekick by HubSpot</u> offer all sorts of email strategies (more on these later). And finally, here's an excellent article by Lincoln Murphy: "<u>7 Sanity Checks for Sending Cold Email</u>".

Email Tracking

Let's talk about what you'll do before, during and after you send your outreach message. Start by following your recipient on Twitter; do this no more than 24 hours before you send your message. This puts a face to a name.

After sending, the big question is, "When should I follow up, and how?" Email tracking will give you the data you need to make an informed decision.

Tracking platforms usually live on your email service or CRM. Though features can vary, most monitor opens, clicks and responses, and they allow you to store and A/B test your email templates. Above all, they track where, when and how your recipients consume your emails.

This technology offers two major advantages:

Connect with context — Contact your recipient at the most relevant time: when they are on your website and thinking about your product.

Measure results — Once you have sent enough emails, you can review your results and revise your templates to optimize performance.

After crunching the data, you might discover one of a few problems. Let's review these:

First, you might notice a low open rate. This might mean that your subject line does not entice your recipient to open the message. This problem should be addressed before others. Try a new subject line; make sure it's personal and straightforward. Envision that you are reconnecting with an acquaintance or an old friend. Stray away from capitalized titles and lines that look like marketing copy.

What if your data shows a low click rate? Basically, the links in your emails aren't getting clicked. This could indicate that your message is too long or uninteresting, or maybe you're sending your emails at an inconvenient time. To fix this, try drafting a shorter and punchier email, improve the value offering, and try sending at a different interval.

Finally, what if you are getting opens and clicks, but those data points aren't materializing responses? This would suggest that either your value proposition isn't strong enough, or the recipient doesn't believe it is worth his or her time to respond. In this case, propose a specific time to talk to them, or decrease the size of your ask. Also, don't be afraid to call them; they've clicked your links and gone to your site. They know who you are and what you do, so this would be a very warm cold call.

Here are a few of the better email tracking services:

Yesware — Very sleek and intuitive, Yesware allows you to use it across your team or as an individual. At the time of this writing, it's available for GMail and Outlook.

ToutApp — A robust platform, ToutApp allows you to set calendar appointments and reminders, and it includes more analytics and features than other services.

Sidekick by Hubspot — Sidekick is a good option if you use other HubSpot products. It has email scheduling, and it populates profiles in your inbox.

If you are new to the idea of email tracking, you might be concerned about privacy. If the practice feels a little weird, remember that you don't have to track everything you send. You can limit it to just the initial outreach message, which is most revealing. If you're a fan of full disclosure, you can include a line at the end of your message, letting your recipient know that the email is tracked, but that no personal information will be shared.

Tracking is especially valuable because your follow-up is just as important—if not more important—than your original message. Your follow-up shows that you are a real person and not a spam bot. Your persistence, within reason, will encourage your prospects to take a look.

Following Up a Cold Email

Let's go into detail on the follow-ups you send after your initial cold email. So we're clear, this is a situation where you're reaching out before you've had a meeting or received a response. There is a full chapter devoted to post-meeting follow-ups later, which will help you guide your prospect through your funnel. Below is an example of a *bad* follow-up email. I probably sent some variation of this before I knew better.

```
Reminder: This is what NOT to do

Subject: Re: Advanced IT Services

Hi [Prospect],

I wanted to follow up regarding our advanced IT
services.  I was wondering if you had a chance to
read the case study I sent a few weeks ago.   If
so, what were your thoughts?

As I mentioned, we offer superior IT services in
the New York area.  Our clients include [Company
A, Company B, Company C].  We were voted as one
of the best providers in the region.

Can we plan on a brief call next week?  If not,
please let me know what works.  I look forward to
learning more about your needs.

Best,

[Salesperson]
```

This email violates many rules we covered. First of all, it's long.

Second, there's little value in it for the recipient. Without providing something useful, you come off as a pesky salesperson.

The email asks two questions that beckon an immediate response: "If so, what were your thoughts?" and "Can we plan on a brief call next week?" These two disparate CTAs, mixed throughout a lengthy message, create too much cognitive legwork for the prospect.

Finally, the ask for a "brief call next week" does not propose a specific time, which makes scheduling a pain.

These problems are glaring, yet I receive messages like this all the time (I bet you do too). Now that we've addressed what makes a bad cold follow-up email, let's look at what goes into a great one.

First, follow up with context! Use email tracking. If you see that the recipient opened your email at a particular time of day, send your follow-up at the same time. If you see opens from different locations, this might indicate that interest is bubbling; don't be afraid to pick up the phone.

Next, limit your CTAs. When you ask too much of a prospect, they don't do anything. After all, they have no obligation to you, and they're probably busy. Make your CTA as frictionless as possible.

Finally, be brief: your follow-up should be no longer than your first email, and generally between two and five sentences. Any longer and the recipient will probably bail after opening. Here's an example:

```
Subject: Re: Advanced IT Services

Hi [Prospect],

I wanted to follow up to make sure this didn't
get lost in the shuffle. If you're interested in
speaking briefly, please let me know how your
calendar looks (tomorrow 1-3p would be great for
me).

If you don't think it would be purposeful, would
you mind directing me to the right person in your
company?

Thanks!

[Salesperson]
```

Lead Generation: Systematize and Outsource

Let's zoom forward a few weeks. You're off and running with lead generation, you've created and optimized email templates for your prospect profiles, and you generally have a grip on your process. At this point, lead generation is taking up a lot of your day, and it's time to start moving it off of your plate.

What are the benefits of outsourcing? For one, it opens up new windows of time. More importantly, it's scalable, and it will let you multiply your efforts. Third, it will help you build organization and delegation skills.

Let's get the lay of the land. There are a multitude of options out there for hiring help. You can hire on an ad-hoc basis, using a service like Upwork. Upwork features a diverse range of talented people, including specialists in lead generation, which is what we're after. If you need a small task completed, you might check out the lower-end services at Fiverr. Also, if you need continuous help on a full- or part-time basis, you can use an online staffing company like Virtual Staff Finder; these services streamline the hiring process, but they require a bigger commitment.

For our purposes, we are going to use Upwork, which is a great starting point because it's much more flexible, and it will help you learn how to manage outsourced workers. It's never too early to get started on Upwork, because once you establish a strong profile and hiring history, you'll be able to attract better talent.

To set up your lead generation machine through outsourcing, we're going to be taking a phased approach. Your process of taking lead generation off your plate is going to happen over the course of a month or so. Here's how the typical hiring process should break down:

Week 1 — Hire a few qualified freelancers.

Week 2 — Test your new hires with a research assignment.

Weeks 3 and 4 — Guide them as they research at full speed.

Week 5 — Unload all remaining lead gen responsibilities.

Let's break the process down a week at a time.

Week 1: Hiring

In week 1, you will write and submit a job post. You can repurpose the below *Job Post Template* for all sorts of hiring situations. Your goal is to hire multiple people so you can determine the best specialist through a test activity in week 2. Based on your needs, you might require more than one freelancer to hit your lead gen quota. If so, you might still prefer to start with one person, to familiarize yourself with the hiring process; that's up to you.

Job Post Template

We seek lead generation specialists for building a list of [###] targeted leads. Our offering is [WHAT YOU DO]. Our goal is to win phone appointments with well-targeted leads, and eventually sales. Success will be measured on the relevance of the leads, and the conversion rate (the rate at which leads agree to an appointment).

Applicants must have excellent research skills, including the ability to track down email addresses.

ENGLISH FLUENCY is required. After this assignment, applicants will be writing and editing email templates.

This is for a one-week, [10-hour] test assignment. If it goes well, we will be able to hire on an ongoing basis at [10 hours] per week.

Familiarity with [YOUR INDUSTRY] is a major plus.

If you wish to apply, please answer the following questions:
-Please describe yourself

```
-What is your proposed rate of pay?

-What is your experience with [YOUR INDUSTRY]?

-What hours are you generally available?

-Tell us about a recent project you completed.

-Please correct the following sentence and place
it at the top of your application:
I is excite apply to position this because I am
lead generation expert.

-Attach a copy of a recent internet speed test

-Lastly, why should we hire you?  Here's a chance
to sell yourself a bit!
We're excited to review your application!
```

Below details how to make an effective online job post. It is based on the Upwork platform, but other websites will require similar information.

On Upwork's "Post a Job" screen, here are some of the important fields you'll need to fill out:

Choose a category — To categorize this job as a lead gen job, select the category "Sales & Marketing", subcategory "Lead Generation".

Give your job a name — Use a simple, straightforward name, such as "Lead Generation for [Your industry]".

Describe the work to be done — Refer to the *Job Post Template*. This gives the freelancer(s) the How and Why of what they'll be doing, an explanation of the test assignment, and a series of questions to help you gauge their suitability.

What skills are needed? — This will vary depending on the platform, but on Upwork the most suitable skills are the following: "lead-generation", "internet-research", "copywriting", "google-docs", "google-spreadsheet", "google-searching", "administrative-support", "data-entry", "linkedin-recruiting" (which will show they know their way around LinkedIn), and "email-handling".

How would you like to pay? — A fixed rate is better, when it's an option. However, this route requires people to estimate how long a task will take, which is hard to do initially. You might try fixed rates once you have built a solid hire history. As you get started, however, an hourly model makes for faster and easier hiring. And don't worry: Upwork has tools to ensure your freelancers are using their billable time effectively, and you can set limits so you don't go over budget.

Estimated duration — Be honest, but it's okay to aim up when estimating your job's duration, for the purpose of selling the opportunity a bit.

Desired experience level — Lead generation freelancers tend to range from about $4.00 to $11.00 per hour. On Upwork, more skilled people will be found under the "intermediate" range. Still, you can find great candidates at $4.00 to $6.50 per hour.

Number of hires — Aim for a bit more than you need. You will filter this number down during the test activity.

As soon as you post the job, you should directly message qualified freelancers to get as many high-quality applications as you can. Search through the site's database for "lead generation". If you wish, search for other skills as well. Then you can use filters such as hourly rate (set it to "$10/hr and below"), freelancer type (use "individual freelancers"; the alternative is through hiring agencies, which can be a hassle), English level ("fluent English"), and hours billed (go for "at least 1,000 hours" for the most experienced people). This will be a great starting point for promising applicants.

Scan the results, reading their introductions, and if it looks good, contact them and invite them to apply for your job. Be super-personalized, and base the message on a job in their recent history if you can. Here is an example:

```
Hi Sally,

Your skills look exceptional!  Based on your work
doing link building back in February, I thought
you might be a good fit for our lead generation
job.   I hope to get the chance to review your
application.  Please let me know if you have any
questions.

Best,

Dan
```

Message about 20-30 relevant and qualified people.

As applicants start rolling in, filter out those who aren't a good fit. You can do this efficiently by ensuring they included the corrected sentence (see *Job Post Template*) at the top of their apps. If you believe they may be qualified, add them to your shortlist.

As you narrow down your shortlist to a few top applicants, message these people and ask them an additional question, such as:

- "Would you mind elaborating on XYZ?"

On top of the extra insight , this conversation lets you gauge the applicant's responsiveness and language proficiency.

Once you've narrowed your shortlist, schedule Skype appointments. Propose a few possible times based on the availability they provided in their applications. In the Skype interview, reiterate some questions, ask candidates to elaborate, and keep factors like signal quality and Internet speed in mind.

One of the best tips is to "hire fast and fire fast". No matter how much you scrutinize applications, you won't know if someone is the right fit until you start working with them. Don't dwell for too long on hiring; just start working with somebody and cut them loose if it's not working out.

Also, only hire people with good reviews. This will let you start with and build upon a foundation of trust.

By the end of week 1, you should have conducted Skype interviews with two or more qualified freelancers, depending on your needs. Bring at least two into the lead generation research test (week 2); remember, you want to have leeway to let one go if necessary.

This process might seem overly complicated, but not to worry: The *Lead Gen Freelancer Blueprint* simplifies the process by laying out specific instructions for your hire. All you have to do is enter your details in the highlighted areas and make any other edits you see fit. From there, you can give it directly to your specialists. The *Blueprint* will help lead us through weeks 2 through 5.

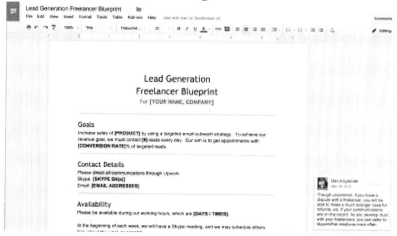

First and foremost, always focus on the Why with your freelancer; they should know the reasoning behind your directions so they can best leverage their talents to help you accomplish your goals.

Goals — Here you might instruct your freelancer as follows: "Increase sales of [Product] by using a targeted email outreach strategy. To achieve our revenue goal, we must contact [#] leads every day. Our aim is to get appointments with [Conversion rate]% of targeted leads."

Ask them if your goals make sense, and if not, ask what is attainable. Before your first Skype meeting, direct them to review the *Blueprint*. This will accelerate the process.

Contact details — Provide your Skype ID and email address(es).

Availability — Specify when you expect your freelancer to be available. Touch base over voice/Skype at the beginning of each week to cover details, answer questions, and offer feedback.

When you get started, you will need to collaborate with them and review their work to ensure they're not going down the wrong path. As they become familiar with your process, you can ease off the heavy oversight.

Tools & Assets — Your freelancers will need a GMail account to use Rapportive, and to work in the Google Docs and spreadsheets.

From this point, your freelancers will be put to the test in week 2, through a lead generation research assignment.

Week 2: Testing

The goal of week 2 is to find all the required information for a set number of leads by the end of the week. Focus on finding leads for a single prospect profile for now, for the sake of simplicity. The video instructions included with the blueprint are from my online course, and demonstrate using LinkedIn for lead generation.

Part A in the blueprint gives a step-by-step approach to finding relevant leads using LinkedIn's advanced search. Once that process is complete, the freelancer will notify you on GChat or Skype. You will then review their progress. An important note is included in all caps: "REVIEW POINT: PLEASE DO NOT CONTINUE UNTIL YOUR WORK IS APPROVED." This will ensure they don't waste valuable time producing data you can't use.

As soon as they can effectively find relevant leads, you can use the second half of the day (or the next day entirely) for email research—part B in the blueprint. Have your freelancer batch their tasks by finding all of the day's leads first, then do all necessary email research for the rest of the day. Schedule the tasks to suit your needs. For email research, tell them not to spend more than five minutes on each email address.

Once the research phase is completed, start sending outreach emails. Remember to use your tracking program to store templates and run A/B tests. Use the same template for a bunch of emails, then switch to a different template for another run, then compare your results.

Weeks 3 and 4: Guiding and Ramping Up

Now it's time to bring your freelancer(s) up to full speed, increasing their daily leads until you hit your quota. Always give them a timeframe, and have them focus on multiple prospect profiles. Remember to keep sending outreach emails yourself so that you can compare their results.

Week 5: Unloading Research and Outreach

By the end of week 5, everything will be in full swing. The freelancer will start sending emails, and modifying them as needed to fit the audience. This must be done carefully, and not too fast, or you won't get the right results. Composing and sending will take some time at first as they learn the process.

They will continue to conduct research, and they'll draft all outreach emails. With your approval, they will send them.

Creating video instructions for your freelancers will make the explanation process much more successful and replicable. You can use programs like Camtasia or ScreenFlow, which are intuitive and easy to use.

Once you trust your freelancer, you can provide them with a company email address. Next, make sure they have access to the email templates; the best place to keep those is in your email tracking platform. Next, have them compose drafts in a Google Doc, which you will review later.

Here's where they're going to get creative by personalizing each one. They'll include the recipient's first name, of course, and then modify the first paragraph to build familiarity. To do that, they can reference recent news articles about the company, LinkedIn developments, or other sources (see "The Stepping Stone Approach" from earlier).

Once they've created about five drafts for different prospects, they'll await your feedback and further instructions. From there they can ramp up to 20 or 30, or more. Once the batch is ready, you'll approve them so they're ready to send.

For the first five emails, they'll make sure to follow a series of steps: load a draft in the compose box, review correctness, make sure all fields are filled in, write a good subject line, BCC your address, make sure the email is tracked (usually by checking a box), enter the target's email address in the "To:" field, then click Send.

After it's sent, they'll log that day's date in the appropriate column in the target list. If you use a CRM, they can do it there, and track it. Also, they'll set a reminder to follow up as appropriate. As we mentioned, the follow-up is often much more important than the initial email, because it shows you're a real person.

Lead Generation: Recap

Lead generation has a lot of moving parts involved. It must be a steady, continuous activity in order to produce results. Thankfully, there are many ways to make it winnable.

First, set ideal daily goals and start mastering your own lead generation process. Do research, craft persuasive templates and systematize your daily activities. Finally, get it all off your plate by outsourcing, using the *Lead Gen Freelancer Blueprint*.

From here, leads will become prospects, and we'll start planning your conversations to achieve your goals in almost any sales situation.

2. The First Conversation

Resources needed:

- *Conversation Blueprint*

- *Pipeline Template*

Learning Objective: Win more deals by planning your conversations.

* * *

I have two important stats for you. The first:

8% of salespeople bring in 80% of all sales (according to Robert Clay, Marketing Wizdom).

How are the successful 8% different from the other 92%? They get their sales process as close to a science as possible by planning their conversations. They leverage the power of word choice and phrasing, edit and test their copy as they go along, and ultimately, win more follow-up appointments. This is key because—here's the second important stat:

80% of lost sales are lost due to lack of follow-up (Ibid).

When it comes to planning and staying on the good side of these trends, a sales script is a valuable tool. The first time someone suggested I use a script, I resisted because I thought it would make me sound fake. Also, to me, every sales situation was a unique hill to climb, so how could a script possibly help?

The truth is, sales situations repeat themselves over and over again. Only the lines and actors change. Your script doesn't have to plan out every word, but it should give the conversation a direction. Although you can't anticipate everything your prospect will say, your script will give you a higher level of confidence and control in almost any sales situation you encounter.

When a new situation arises, you will update your script so you can address it properly in the future. Before long, your process will become automatic, and you won't have to stare at a document every time you're on a call or in a meeting.

In this chapter, you will create a script using the *Conversation Blueprint*. It will help you lay out the right phrases, and keep track of your progress and goals. A sample script is included as well, which you can use as inspiration.

The Conversation Blueprint

Dan Englander, www.SalesSchema.com

GOAL of 1st meeting

_____

GOAL of 2nd meeting

_____

GOAL of 3rd meeting

_____

Average Sales Cycle:

This chapter deals with the first sales conversation. Your cold lead agrees to this meeting as a short discussion about their needs. In this conversation, you will fully qualify your prospect and understand their buying situation. Then you will give a customized pitch that aligns your offering to the needs you uncovered. Your pitch will be memorable through the use of audio and/or visual assets. Finally, you will naturally transition to a follow-up appointment.

The topics in this chapter are presented in chronological order, based on the general flow of the first sales conversation. The design of your conversation will intersperse your probing questions with useful information for your prospect. This ensures you will have a conversation — not an interrogation — and will help you build trust as a consultant, instead of just a salesperson.

The Conversation Blueprint

This document will guide you through your meetings. It is impossible to be exact in mapping out your sales conversations — every one is different — so this document should reflect a "typical" situation for you.

Start by defining an ideal goal for each meeting. Identify the length of your "Average Sales Cycle" and write that in as well.

Next, fill out your likelihood legend. Define each percentage block of your sales cycle from 10% to 100%. You don't have to fill out all ten blocks, only the key milestones. Here is a general guideline:

- 10%: They agree to a conversation.

- 20%: They have a budget.

- 30%: They have a budget and a schedule.

- **40%:** All of the above and decision within two weeks or less.

- **50%:** All of the above and we're on their shortlist.

- **60%:** All of the above and we're recommended to the team or superiors.

- **90%:** They verbally commit to us, but nothing is in writing.

- **100%:** Contract is signed, and they are now customers.

We have completed the first part of the *Conversation Blueprint*. We will revisit it later as we proceed through the first sales conversation.

The Pipeline Template

In addition to the *Conversation Blueprint*, the *Pipeline Template* will help you monitor sales progress. It will help you visualize and keep track of all your prospects in one place.

A	B	C	D	E	F	G
Prospect	Likelihood	Estimated Spend	Value	Date Created	Last Activity	Next Steps
ACME	20.00%	$20,000.00	$4,000.00	12/1/2014	12/15/2014	Followup call to discuss proposal.
Kramerica Industries	10.00%	$30,000.00	$3,000.00	11/1/2014	12/15/2014	Find out best next steps.
SalesSchema	40.00%	$40,000.00	$16,000.00	11/16/2014	12/17/2014	Set up conference call with founder.
		Total value	$23,000.00			

In the first column, enter your prospect's name. Next, enter the likelihood of closing the sale, based on your likelihood legend; then enter an estimate of the dollar value of the sale (the estimated spend). The value of your prospect, then, is the likelihood multiplied by the estimated spend. You can use this to calculate the total value of your pipeline at any given time, and eventually even forecast your future revenue.

Two fields, "Date Created" and "Latest Activity," will tell you how long the prospect has been in your sales pipeline and how long since an action was last taken. Don't let too much time pass without trying to push them up in your pipeline. If necessary, you may want to "go for a no" and get them out of your pipeline so you can focus your time on better opportunities (a concept we'll tackle later). The "Next Steps" field is important, so you always know what should come next in the process. This column will tell you if the situation has stagnated so you can rekindle interest as needed.

How to Start Sales Conversations

Most people make buying decisions to solve a problem or alleviate pain. The challenge is that many people often can't identify their problems, or they misdiagnose them. By the end of this chapter, you will understand proven techniques to help you understand your prospect's problems.

But first, how do you start your conversation? You can't just start pelting people with questions; you must begin by building rapport. You'll need to pick up on and respond to explicit and implied social cues, especially at the beginning of the conversation.

Start the conversation with basic pleasantries:

- "Hi, how are you?"

- "How's the weather in Omaha?"

You might also choose to recall something from your email conversation. Keep your ears open, listen carefully and ask yourself questions like these:

- How fast is this person talking?

- How stressed or calm do they sound?

- Are their speaking habits slow and comfortable, or quick and nervous?

These implied cues will help you direct your questions. If they sound tense or impatient, you should be specific and relevant, or they may get impatient and tune you out. Your questions should be offered with context and your pitch should be especially short and punchy.

If your prospect is pleasant and meandering, then don't be afraid to match them and slow things down. Living and working in New York increases your pace, and it's been comical how much I've had to slow things down based on my prospects.

Explicit cues will help you find out how much time you're working with. Nothing throws you off more than discovering that your prospect has to jump off of the call prematurely, for whatever reason. Ask them directly: "We'll need about 15 minutes, does that work for you?"

Take the pressure off your prospect by padding your tough questions. More importantly, get them talking. Open with phrases like:

- "If you don't mind me asking, . . ."

- "Just wondering, but . . ."

- "Would you tell me more about XYZ?"

Qualify Your Prospect

The first thing to focus on when qualifying your prospects is their **previous experience**. If they purchased from a company like yours in the past, they will likely have specific expectations. But, even if they're new to your industry, they are sure to have concerns about the solution in general, as well as your offering, and they will need some guidance. Find out about their previous experience early, because it will determine the rest of the conversation.

Here are some example questions (you will find these and more questions in the *Conversation Blueprint*):

- "Have you ever hired a company like ours? What was the experience like? What would you like to improve?"

- "What has been your strategy when it comes to email marketing [or IT, or anything else]? How well has that worked?"

Next, find out about your prospect's **individual considerations**. These focus on the person you're talking to directly, not other stakeholders. You want them talking about themselves; "I", not "we". Your main contact will probably have sway in the buying decision, so you want to target them, personally, by finding out their pressures, goals, and responsibilities. Would they like to grow their business? Save their job? Get a raise? Try to find out.

- "What responsibilities are on you, personally, when it comes to XYZ?"

- "Can you tell me a little about your day when it comes to XYZ?"

- "I hope you don't mind me asking, but what would fall on your shoulders when it comes to this engagement?"

- "Just wondering, but what are you most concerned about personally?"

Finally, you want to uncover **political considerations**. Find out how other people in the organization affect your prospect's challenges and aspirations. By doing this, you'll learn how other personalities might affect the buying decision. Here is a set of example questions:

- "To make sure I get you the right details, I'm wondering, what other stakeholders will be involved in this engagement? What roles will they have?

- "If you don't mind me asking, who are you most concerned about pleasing? What's most important to them?"

Action Item #2

Complete the "Problems" section of the *Conversation Blueprint*. Use a stream-of-consciousness approach to write as many questions as you can for unveiling previous experience, individual considerations and political considerations.

Finding the "Actual" Budget

Whereas we previously discussed the past and present, we now shift our focus to the future.

Have you ever shopped for a big-ticket item, and been asked the question, "What's your budget?" How did you feel? You likely tensed up a bit. You may have felt like the salesperson was trying to see how much they could squeeze out of you. It's also possible you didn't give it much thought, or maybe you didn't know if the number in your head was reasonable. Many salespeople save discussion of money for the very end, when people are ready to end the call. Treating the budget question as an afterthought often produces vague or unhelpful answers.

To avoid this situation, integrate numbers, price, target return on investment (ROI), goals, and other similar considerations into the beginning of the call. Ask about general business goals, then transition into the prospect's ideal ROI; with this, you will reveal a feasible budget, and know if you're the right fit.

Some business goal questions include:

- "What would a win look like in this case?"

- "How will you be monitoring success?"

- "What needs to happen for you to consider the engagement successful?"

Once you have enough goal-related information, it's time to dive further into the numbers. Depending on your product, figuring out ROI might be straightforward, or it might be complex. Your questions may be difficult to answer, so be sure to pad them:

- "How many leads would our offering need to bring in for you to consider it a success?"

- "I know this might be a tough question, but what is your typical close rate?"

- "What was your average user rating last quarter? How much are you looking to improve that rating?"

Next, delve into what these numbers mean. In reference to the numbers the prospect provided to the questions above, you might ask:

- "Was that an increase from previous periods?"

- "Is this goal a major increase? How ambitious do you think it is? Why or why not?"

These inquiries are difficult, and it's likely that your prospect won't have immediate answers. You might even stump them completely. If so, help them out by putting numbers on the blank slate of their minds:

- "Hypothetically, if our offering brought in five leads per month, would that be a win?"

- "Next quarter, if you got 50 5-star reviews, would that be a success?"

- "If you improved your earnings per click by $3 during your next campaign, would that be a major improvement?"

Once you have learned about your prospect's goals, you will need to translate them into dollars so you can determine ROI. Why? Because you'll be paid in dollars. By going through this exercise with all your prospects, you will determine if your offering is the right fit, save a lot of time, and invest yourself in the right opportunities.

Help your prospect look at the big picture by turning their goals into tangible financial outcomes over a particular period of time. There are moving parts involved, but here's how you might pull everything together:

- "You mentioned your close rate is around 10%, you're going for 50 new leads next month, and your average deal size is $1,000. So is it fair to say that $5,000 is a good rough estimate for next month's revenue goal?"

The math in the example above is somewhat clear, but what if your solution is more detached from dollars generated? In that case, you'll need to convert the relative improvement your product provides into money. Focus on what your prospect has spent in similar situations in the past:

- "If you don't mind me asking, roughly how much does it cost you when this problem happens?"

After that, find out what your prospect is willing to spend to solve the problem. Don't ask them directly, but lead them with a question like this:

- "From our experience, that problem tends to cost our customers $X per month. Would you say that roughly matches your situation? If not, about how far off am I?"

Any information you gather when it comes to the numbers will be extremely helpful, so always ask these questions, even if they feel uncomfortable at first. Gauging your prospect early on will allow you to invest yourself in the best opportunities.

Action Item #3

Create your own "Goals --> ROI --> Budget" funnel in your *Conversation Blueprint*. Fill out questions and scenarios to put numbers on the blank page of your prospect's mind. If this task is difficult for you, start by making a list of relevant metrics, then figure out how you can translate them into dollars. If you're still hitting a wall, try getting input from a past customer, and ask how they have been measuring success.

Make the Pitch

You have asked a lot of tough questions, so now it's time to give your prospect some details about your offering. This is your pitch, and you will craft it in a persuasive and memorable way, but it will be a natural part of the conversation—not a detached, overly-rehearsed sales spiel. You will tailor your pitch based on the problems and goals you uncovered.

First, ask your prospect what information would be most helpful:

- "What details are you looking to get at this point?"

This will ensure your presentation doesn't leave anything out. In particular, make sure you include at least a rough estimate of pricing. It's important to get a reaction on price during the first conversation; otherwise, you'll risk wasting time on people who can't afford you.

If they ask about price before you're ready, respond somewhat like this:

- "There's a range associated with different options. To offer context, I'd like to tell you a bit more about us, and then I'll go through the possibilities. Does that work for you?"

Many salespeople (myself included before I knew better) focus their pitch almost exclusively on their features, benefits and differentiators. While these details are important, they often fail to build an emotional connection, and busy people tend to forget them. To be memorable, it really helps to build an emotional connection, and a great way to do that is by focusing on the Why. The first line of your pitch should answer the following question: "Why do you do what you do?" For example, this was my opening line from my successful pitch: "We started IdeaRocket because we realized it's important that people understand your message quickly."

After you've covered the Why, answer this question: "What makes you different?" This is more than a rigid list of differentiators. Explain what sets you apart in a way that's tied to solving your prospect's problems. As such, your differentiators won't necessarily be the same every time. Early in the conversation, start making mental connections between problems and how your differentiators will solve them. Emphasize the most relevant ones.

From my pitch, I'd often say, "Our main differentiator is our high-quality approach, which we are able to achieve because we have access to many talented artists here in New York." If the prospect complained about a previous experience with an uncommunicative vendor, I might say, "Our main differentiator is our streamlined broadcast production process. This involves daily status reports and detailed timelines."

Next, drive the points home by answering this question: "Why do these differences matter?" In other words, why are your differentiators important? I would say, "In my experience, video quality matters because it's the first thing website visitors see. For our clients, it ends up being shared more than any other asset, and it almost always becomes a major brand fixture."

During your pitch, you have to make arguments and recommendations. Given your bias, how do you maintain trust with your prospect? One word: phrasing.

Words affect us instinctively. One powerful word you might want to work into your pitch vocabulary is "because". Its strength was documented by social psychologist Ellen Langer, in a study in *The Journal of Personality and Social Psychology*. Let's call it the "copy machine study".

In Langer's experiment, she asked to cut in line to use a copy machine. She tested three different ways of asking people, and recorded the results:

For the first test, she said the following: "Excuse me, I have five pages. May I use the Xerox machine?" 60% of people said yes.

For the second test, she said: "Excuse me, I have five pages. May I use the Xerox machine because I'm in a rush?" 94% said yes.

Finally, the most surprising outcome came from the third test, when she said: "Excuse me, I have five pages. May I use the Xerox machine because I have to make some copies?" 93% of people said yes.

The word "because" is so persuasive that the reason behind it doesn't matter—in Langer's experiment, the latter justification (". . . because I have to make some copies") is irrelevant.

Another powerful phrase to sprinkle into your conversations is "in my experience". Your prospect knows deep down that you understand your offering or your industry better than they do, but they may struggle to believe your statements because of your clear bias. You still have to make recommendations and assertions, but you can curtail skepticism by using the phrase "in my experience", which no one can disprove.

Before you dive into your pitch, consider the situation. Who else, or what else, is vying for your prospect's attention? It is almost certain that your prospect is busy — we all are. They deal with regular office distractions, and they might be comparing you to competitors.

Have you ever had to make a buying decision during a busy work day? If so, you probably made a list. You disqualified the obvious bad fits, and from there, the remaining options might have blurred together. In this situation, the most memorable contestant often wins.

One way to make your pitch stickier is with quick and punchy visuals. They will enhance your pitch without drawing it out. Focus each on a key differentiator. "Less is more" should be your mantra here. A few simple ideas include a two-to-three-minute Prezi presentation, a product tour or case study, or a short but relevant video.

After you've gone through your pitch and used visuals to advance it, provide your prospect with pricing information. Most likely, if they don't know about pricing yet, they'll be itching for it. Provide a relatively loose range, or exclude a certain "x factor" to encourage a later conversation. Always make sure to get an immediate reaction. Here's one way to present it:

- "Our pricing for the website would be in the realm of $5,000, but I'd like to learn more about your design needs so I can get you harder numbers. How does that resonate with you?"

- "Based on what we talked about, my initial recommendation would be for us to create a mid-sized widget. Depending on the specs, this would range from $10-15 thousand. How does that sound to you?"

Let's say you get one of these responses:

"Sounds great." — This doesn't necessarily mean you're in the end zone. Keep digging to find out where you stand. Follow up with questions like these:
- "Just to make sure I don't waste your time, is that range in line with what you were planning?"

- "Just curious, but what similar investments are you making now?"

"Sorry, that's too high for us." — They express a concern about your pricing, compared to what they had in mind. Respond by saying:
- "Thanks for letting me know. If you don't mind me asking, what general range are you aiming for?"

We'll go into addressing common objections later, as well as giving your prospect helpful tools to frame the decision in your favor.

Action Item #4

Fill out the "Pitch" section of the *Conversation Blueprint*. Focus on why you do what you do, what makes you different, and why this difference matters. Practice reading it aloud and edit it as needed.

Next, get constructive criticism from a friend or coworker. This is extremely important.

Finally, jot down a few ideas for visual assets to accompany your pitch, and when you have time, try creating one of them.

Transition to Follow-Up Conversations

How to Make Urgency Drive Sales

It's time to learn more about your prospect's situation, including their schedule. Now that you have solicited information about your offering, you'll be in a better spot to ask further questions. Prospects with a schedule are obviously more valuable than those with vague plans.

Here are a few questions for better understanding timeframe:

- "When might be an ideal time to take something like this on?"

- "So I can make sure to get you the right details on time, by when are you looking to select a provider?"

- "By when would you like to get started?"

- "By when would you like to be finished?"

If your prospect gives you a delay, you need to diagnose the reason for the holdup. Find out if it's a legitimate delay, or if it's a polite way of blowing you off. Ask questions and use your instincts. Here's an example:

- "If you don't mind me asking, how will your situation change between now and then?"

They might answer with what sounds like a legitimate reason, but make sure you listen for their tone and other subtle cues. Depending on how they respond, either take their word for it or, if you're skeptical, try to get them to tell you "no" by proposing a follow-up:

- "Before I set a calendar appointment to follow up, I just want to make sure I'm not wasting your time. Should I go ahead and set an appointment?"

Or you can be more direct:

- "Just to make sure I don't waste your time, is this a nice way of letting me know you're not interested? If that's the case, it would be no problem at all."

These are difficult questions to ask because you're setting yourself up for possible rejection and awkwardness. But it is far worse to waste time with people who will never buy from you. If they do admit (or imply) that there's no immediate need, don't kick them out of your pipeline forever, but you should definitely de-prioritize them.

If you feel like there's still a good possibility, remember that your prospect is likely delaying because they are busy. If they are juggling lots of different projects, they might (for example) know they have to get started with you in Q3, but a few months in the future might be an eternity in their minds. In situations like these, it's extremely helpful to tie your prospect to the calendar with the help of a timeline.

To set up your timeline, first tell them how long it will take to get them set up. This process might include contracts, deposits, interviews, and discovery. Next, make it clear how long it will take to realize the value your offering promises, including key milestones and deadlines. This will help them visualize the process, and will help accelerate your sales cycle. Later you'll get help from timeline creation tools.

Action Item #5

Complete the "Schedule" section of your *Conversation Blueprint*. Focus on questions that will reveal the ideal time for your prospect to get started. Also, lay out a method for diagnosing delays, and don't be afraid to push for a "no".

How to Address Objections

Many sales methods talk about "handling" objections as if they are tiny fires that can be extinguished with a splash of water. The truth is, some people will be right for your offering, and others won't. You should certainly work to overcome objections, but let's ditch the idea that there's a silver bullet for all forms of push-back. Instead, it's better to anticipate common objections and prevent them from arising in the first place. Your qualifying questions should help you understand your prospect's situation such that you can address many concerns before they come up. But what happens when objections do arise?

You've interviewed your prospect and made your pitch. If there are objections, here is when they are likely to rise to the surface. Up until now, it's probably been a positive conversation. Following an objection, the atmosphere becomes a bit tense; if you panic and start spouting off counterclaims, it will almost certainly makes things worse. Instead, take the pressure off. Reduce the tension by making it clear that you accept their objection, and admit to them that you might not be the right fit. For example, you could say:

- "That's a valid point. I'm not sure yet if we're a fit, and if not, I know I can help out by making the right recommendation. But there are a few things I am wondering about regarding the in-house solution you mentioned. . . ."

Once you acknowledge their concern, you can proceed to learn more about the reason for the objection. For example:

- "Have you had a chance to do an analysis of the hours and costs that go into using your in-house solution?"

- "By the way, how did you go about creating that solution?"

- "Have you had a chance to check out the case studies from companies in your industry that switched from in-house to a professional solution? Whether you go with us or not, I think it will be helpful to review those. I'll send them over. . . ."

If the objection derives from doubt that their problems are serious enough to justify your solution, make sure the problems' implications are not getting lost in the noise.

Reiteration and a little more prying can help bring your prospect's pain to the surface:

- "Just to make sure I understand your issues, it's taking your team way too long to prepare your reports each week. I'm wondering, what does this mean in terms of your team's service to your customers? How is that affected?"

If the problems don't create a need for your solution, then see what else you can find. Do some research or ask more questions. After you uncover the biggest problem, focus on the outcome. Ask what reality your prospect will enjoy if they work with you:

- "If you were able to reduce your team's report creation hours by 50%, what would that mean for you? Would that mean taking on more customers? If so, how many?"

Price is another common objection. We touched on this, but let's dig deeper. Your prospect says that the price is higher than they had in mind. You might say:

- "Thanks for letting me know. If you don't mind me asking, what range are you aiming for?"

From there, explore how far off you really are. If possible, reduce the scope of the solution. Never discount the price without accordingly reducing the scope; you will immediately lose trust if your prospect perceives your pricing to be arbitrary. Be upfront and easygoing about what you're doing. You can say:

- "I'm not trying to reconnoiter things to meet your budget, but I want to make sure you have all the options. With that in mind, would you entertain our economy offering at $X lower price?"

Also, take money out of the equation to make sure that budget is the real issue. Try asking this question:

- "If money were not an issue at all, what would be the best possible outcome?"

Based on the response, demonstrate how you would provide that outcome. Once that's clear and you're in alignment, then ask:

- "Has this situation happened before, where someone had the right solution but it was over budget? What did you do?"

Another possibility is that your prospect is too early in the buying process to have an appropriate budget in mind. In this case, they will almost certainly be looking at competitors, and you might as well be the one to guide their comparison. Give them the names of your most relevant competitors, and provide useful information that, while unbiased, accentuates your strengths. This will build trust and confidence around your offering, and you'll be likely to win in the end. As an example, I will cover my often-used *Competitive Comparison Chart* later on.

Finally, if your prospect's budget is considerably low, don't be afraid to back away a bit. You can simply say:

- "With that budget in mind, we're probably not the right fit. Our focus is on high quality."

If someone is truly under your range, move on. But do what you can to point them in the right direction. They might circle back to you later if you give them a good experience.

You might choose to refer them to a lower-cost provider in exchange for a commission. In this case, sell your partner a bit. You can say something like this:

- "Based on my experience, I think our friends at ACME will provide the best quality for your budget."

If your prospect doesn't have a schedule or keeps delaying, diagnose the hold-up. Make sure it's legitimate, and that there's still a need and a budget. Next, put timing in front of them. If they seem to have no sense of urgency, emphasize the delay between their start date and when they will begin to enjoy the value of your offering. A timeline is a great tool for illustrating this point.

Action Item #6

In the *Conversation Blueprint*, complete the "Responding to Objections" section. These don't necessarily have to be the examples we covered here. Make your objections specific to your experience. Write responses that take the pressure off and explore all opportunities.

Find the Decision-Makers

How often have you heard this from prospects?: "Thanks for all the information. Give us some time to pore over it and we'll get back to you." Many opportunities will end here if you are not proactive about securing a follow-up appointment. Here's that important stat again:

80% of lost sales are lost due to lack of follow-up.

From this section you will know how to unveil your prospect's decision-making process, guide it appropriately, and transition naturally to a follow-up appointment.

Prying into the decision-making process happens most comfortably at the end of the conversation. The most successful follow-up meetings tend to be those where you're steering the process by offering helpful information to the deciding parties. Many sales methods insist that you must always reach the decision-maker—and that's certainly ideal—but you must pursue them with the right touch.

As an example, let's say your first point of contact is an underling—we'll call her Mary. Mary will be presenting the details of your offering to her superior, and she let you know what her boss values in a vendor. You do your best to set up a meeting with Mary and her superior, but to no avail; Mary wants to be the liaison, and despite your best efforts it appears you are stuck with her. As a gatekeeper, she carries a lot of weight in the buying decision. Some sales methods would advocate going over Mary's head, but would that violation of trust be worth the potential reward? Absolutely not.

It's not worth pushing for the ultimate decision-maker at the expense of alienating other stakeholders, unless you have nothing to lose. If that gatekeeper is being unresponsive and you think you have a shot at winning over the superior, then go for it. However far you rise up the company chain, make sure you completely understand the decision-making process by asking good questions of all stakeholders.

There has been a lot of give and take thus far in the conversation, but the decision-making questions are clearly asked for your benefit. With that in mind, soften them and be especially courteous:

- "If you don't mind me asking, how is a decision like this usually made?"

- "After you collect all the information you need, what happens next? Will you be presenting it to a larger group? Will you be selecting a provider to talk about with your group? To get you the most relevant background information, what is most important to them?"

- "Will you be presenting several providers, or just one?"

Any answers you can get to questions like these will be valuable. Next you will stay involved by making yourself useful. The overall goal is to add value and make things easier for the deciders, and a great way to do that is by offering them a tangible resource for their next discussion:

- "We covered a lot of ground on our call, and in my experience, details can get lost in translation. With that in mind, would it be helpful if I joined you and your team via a conference line when you talk about this?"

- "Whether you choose us or not, I think that a timeline will be helpful so you can understand the process and avoid a time crunch. Can we connect briefly next week so I can run a draft schedule by you?"

If your prospect declines your follow-up request, inform them that you will be checking back in a few days to a week:

- "I'll plan on following up with you on Wednesday morning to discuss best next steps."

This persistence can be powerful because they know you will be following up no matter what, and they will be more likely to give you a straight decision. You may not get the ideal answer, but you will certainly get *an* answer, and you will keep the process moving forward.

To stay ahead of the follow-up game, here are some tips. First of all, always know what your next step will be before the meeting, and have backup options in mind as your prospect's story unfolds. Decide what makes sense as a next step, and direct the conversation accordingly.

Finally, remember to always arrange and send calendar appointments in real time as you talk to your prospect. This will help ensure your follow-ups stay locked down:

- "Since my schedule tends to run away from me, is it okay if we get something on the calendar now? How about Tuesday at 2:00 p.m.?"

Action Item #7

In the *Conversation Blueprint*, complete the "Decision-Making Process" section. Write questions that fit your industry and your speaking habits.

Also, for the "Follow-Up Appointment" section, write a few ideas for transitioning to a follow-up. Base your ideas on typical situations you've faced in the past.

The First Conversation: Recap

You're well on your way to winning on your important calls and meetings. At this point you should have most of your *Conversation Blueprint* filled out. Here are some important points from this chapter:

- Stay organized when monitoring your progress with prospects. The *Pipeline Template* will help.

- During your first call, balance your questions with useful information; maintain a conversation, not an interrogation.

- Find problems by focusing on previous experience, individual considerations and political considerations.

- Help your prospect reveal their actual budget by identifying an ideal return on investment. Help them out with hypothetical scenarios and put numbers on the blank page in their minds.

- Give your pitch: Go beyond benefits and features, and focus on creating an emotional impact; shed light on why you do what you do, what makes you different, and why this difference is important. Use quick and punchy visuals to stay memorable.

- Give pricing details while keeping the conversation open, and get an immediate reaction.

- Find the ideal schedule your prospect requires for an offering like yours. If you get a delay, diagnose if it's legitimate or a blow-off. If necessary, give them a timeline and tie them to the calendar.

- Avoid objections by learning about your prospect's needs before you present your offering. When objections do arise, accept them, ask questions and explore all opportunities.

- Transition to a follow-up appointment, and stay involved by being continuously helpful.

The next section continues the process, focusing on follow-up appointments. You will learn all about how to win the big "yes" during the second, third or hundredth meeting. This will involve specific strategies, templates and other tools to give you a serious edge.

3. Following Up and Closing the Sale

Resources Needed:

- *Conversation Blueprint*

- *Unresponsiveness Template*

Learning objective: Win follow-up appointments and avoid the pitfalls responsible for over 80% of all lost deals.

* * *

At this point, you've gone through a lengthy process to land a meeting, and you don't want this opportunity to slip through your fingers because you forgot to lock down a next step. As we discussed, the best way to secure a follow-up appointment is to make a mutually-confirmed calendar appointment in real time.

What happens if you don't set up the appointment? Most likely, you will defer to asking, "Is it OK if I call you back next week?" and the prospect may say, "Yeah, go for it." When the time comes, you will probably find that this person is unreachable. However, most people do not neglect their calendar appointments. Maybe they say, "I'm super-busy next week and I'm not sure what my schedule will look like. Can you follow up with me then?" Don't fall for it; again, if they don't commit, you may become an afterthought. Use their busy schedule as the reason for leaning on the calendar:

- "I know the feeling. My schedule's almost completely filled up next week too. Since I have my calendar in front of me now, why don't we see if we can get something scheduled? How about Thursday at 3?"

On some level, everyone fears rejection. You may worry about being too pushy. This is normal. But at the end of the day, you need to secure a follow-up, and the best way to prevent anxiety is by planning things out. Make sure your transition fits your speaking habits. Write it out, practice and edit it as needed. From there, incorporate your transition into every call and meeting until it becomes automatic.

Now that you've secured a follow-up, what are you supposed to talk about in the second, third, and later meetings? Thankfully, the process remains pretty much the same. Always make sure to balance your questions with useful information until closing the sale is the next logical step. We touched on a few tools you can discuss with your prospect, like a timeline, case study or comparison chart, and we will cover those in detail in chapter 5. But for now, let's focus on a few great tactics for moving the sales process forward during your follow-up meetings.

Connect the Comrades

Before you adopt this strategy, make sure you're dealing with a real opportunity. Your prospect should have an acceptable budget and a significant need that your offering can fulfill. If those things are in place, you can connect the comrades by getting your prospect talking to a like-minded peer from your organization. For example, if you're dealing with an owner of a company, try to get your company's owner involved. You can apply this strategy for all sorts of positions, including engineers, accountants, lawyers, project managers and many others.

What are the benefits of this approach? First and foremost, it builds rapport, comfort and trust on a much deeper level than you can achieve alone. It introduces someone into the process who can intimately relate to what the prospect goes through. Second, it ups the ante. It conveys that you are more than just a salesperson; you are part of a team. Once your prospect recognizes that others on your end are involved, they will be more willing to accept follow-up appointments and less likely to flake. Furthermore, you can use this approach to encourage involvement from higher-level decision-makers on your prospect's side. Using your knowledge of their decision-making process as a guide, set up the next meeting with something like this:

- "Since I think my colleague's insight into our development process will be helpful, I think it would be a good idea if your lead developer joined as well. Would you mind looping him in?"

Introducing a new voice keeps the process fresh, compelling and forward-moving. At this point, your prospect might worry that the next call will be repetitive (and thus, a waste of time), or, having received pricing on the previous call, they may fear being pushed into a decision. Connecting the comrades presents a new opportunity to offer value.

How would you set this up on your side? Before you arrange anything, make sure the opportunity is worth both your and your colleague's time. Next, figure out who you have access to on your team, and give them a heads-up at least a few days in advance. The colleague does not have to be a salesperson, but they should be able to carry a conversation with a stranger. It's preferable if they're in a client-facing role. Give your colleague some rough details on what you expect to talk about. Let them know that you will lead the call, and that you will introduce them. A couple hours before the meeting, give your colleague an in-depth briefing on the prospect and their company. This will ensure the information is fresh. Also, have your colleague prepare some questions for the meeting, or you can draft up questions yourself. You shouldn't script the whole conversation, but a few questions will generate a conversation.

You set up this meeting, but what will you talk about? At the start, be sure to reiterate some key details from your previous meeting. Continue to qualify your prospect, and make sure you understand their buying situation and if anything has changed. Here are a few things you could ask:

- "By the way, how did our pricing resonate with your team?"

- "What are your thoughts on the case studies I sent over?"

- "At this point, by when should the project be done?"

Next, introduce your colleague, and use the core of the call to continue to educate your prospect. Get your colleague and your prospect on the same page, and be sure your colleague is asking some questions. Your colleague should learn about the prospect's challenges and goals from a like-minded perspective. If you like, you can reuse a few questions you have asked before — they will be appropriate in the new context—but try digging deeper to understand needs.

From there, focus on showing your prospect what the improved outcome will look like. Give specific ideas and insights. Discuss a relevant case study, sketch out something over Skype, or hash over specific recommendations. Give them a taste of what it will be like working with you. Allow your prospect and your colleague to contribute to the ideas, to inspire a sense of ownership in the potential engagement.

In general, make the engagement real, though still unofficial. The next logical step will be officializing it by signing the papers, submitting an invoice and moving forward. Put a specific recommendation down on paper (i.e., email), memorializing it. Your next follow-up appointment can be for you and your prospect to discuss the recommendation, and make sure to meet before the prospect presents the recommendation to other decision-makers. Don't be afraid to talk about price again, and always lock down a mutually-confirmed calendar appointment.

Sometimes, prospects will ask if they can speak with your superior or colleagues before you're ready to offer up your people. They might think they will get better information, or that they will have a better negotiating position. Do not grant their request unless you believe the opportunity is worth the time of you and your team. To find out if that's the case, you might ask:

- "Just curious, but what would you like to accomplish with this meeting?"

If you do have to say "no", let them know that your colleague or superior is extremely busy, and keep deferring as needed until you decide that person should be in the loop. This builds up the value of your team's time, which can be beneficial.

The Silver Bullet for Getting a Response

What if you secure a follow-up appointment, but your prospect flakes? What if you get repeated apologies and deferrals, and it appears you're being blown off?

The *Unresponsiveness Template* is a simple email that will compel a response in almost any situation. As always, your emails should be tailored to your voice. When templates are used verbatim on a large scale, they tend to lose their power.

```
Hi [Prospect],

You're probably quite busy, or somehow my last
email didn't reach you, so I thought I'd reach
out again and check in as to where we are with
the project.

I'm    sure    you    realize    that    I'm    being
professionally  persistent,  but  if  you  are  not
interested  or  things  have  changed,  I  would
appreciate  you  letting  me  know  so  we  can
determine what the next best step should be.

Look forward to your thoughts.

Best,

[You]
```

This email is great because it's honest and direct. You fall on your sword by admitting that you're being persistent. You're not asking them to buy or take any other major action; all you're asking is that they respect your time. This email almost always gets results. Even if you get a "no", it will move the process forward.

Negotiations

The art of negotiation is greatly exaggerated in TV and movies, where the most dominant and demanding player is portrayed as the winner. However, you will soon learn that a great negotiator is quite a departure from that image.

You might enter a negotiation when you are shortlisted as a provider, or a certain prospect is interested in you. At this point, you are far enough along in the sales process that you've found someone who is likely a good fit for your offering.

Before you start a negotiation, be mindful of areas in your policies where you can be flexible, and those where you cannot. Price is a big one, but there are others. Up until now, you may have only provided a rough price estimate. As you learn more about needs, get more specific about price and gauge your prospect's reaction.

Before you start a negotiation, never offer a price range. If, for example, you mention a range of "between X and Y," the customer won't settle until they get X. Be upfront about the areas where you can't budge. This will help you avoid time-wasting and aggravation.

You should also make sure that every concession you make has a reciprocation attached. If you are not firm about this, your pricing will seem arbitrary, which will inspire distrust.

When negotiations collapse, this is usually the reason. Here's a basic example of reciprocation:

- "If I'm willing to do X, would you be willing to entertain Y?"

You may worry that your prospect has all the leverage in the negotiation, and that you will have to kowtow to make a deal. Maybe, but probably not. You likely have more leverage than you think. Remember: Your prospect has already come this far with you, and if you don't bend they know they might face the exact same issues (or a different set of problems entirely) with your competitors.

What if they dangle the threat of engaging a competitor over your head during a negotiation? If they try this tactic, then recommend that they do an honest comparison, and give them the tools and resources to do so.

During negotiation, you can enjoy liberation and leverage when you remove yourself from the role of decision-maker. This is key. You will be playing the role of a sales peon, and your mantra should be, *"What do we have to do to make this work?"*

This should not be too difficult. From the start, you've been a helpful consultant, guiding your prospect through the ins and outs of your offering. And after all this time spent trying to lead them to "yes", it would be off-putting to suddenly be the one saying "no". Let someone else fill that role, like your boss or a department in your company. For example, if your prospect says, "Can you guys give us net 60 instead of net 30 payment terms?" don't say yes or no; say something like:

- "I can't promise that, but I'll check with our finance department. Because I'm sure they'll ask me, would you be willing to entertain a 75% deposit up front if I can get you those terms?"

This is ideal for two reasons. First, you are deferring the decision; and second, you're proposing a reciprocation.

Deferring power puts you in a more sympathetic position because you show that you are subject to your company's annoying bureaucracy—a scenario to which your prospect might very well relate. They might be worried about paperwork and jumping through corporate hoops to set up the deal, so they'll be more likely to cooperate with you. Do them a favor and make the setup process as smooth as possible for them. Try to understand their hurdles by asking what needs to happen for you to get locked in, and how you can make the process easier. If you are proactive about this, you will be much more likely to win.

Also, remove ego and emotion from negotiations. Don't challenge their decisions by saying things like, "This is the best price for your industry," "You're passing up a great opportunity," or, "You're making a big mistake." In the ensuing battle of emotions, no one will win (certainly not you). If you have negotiated as far as you can go, it can be difficult, but it might be best to walk away. Remember that they will still have to negotiate with other vendors, and you may well wind up being the best solution in the end. They may also try to hang rejection over your head as a last ditch tactic, in hopes that you will offer a lower price or another concession. Be prepared for these situations, and don't take them personally. If you bring ego into the equation, they might go out of their way to not work with you, even if they know it's against their best interests.

The Natural Close

Many sales methods promote an "Always Be Closing" (ABC for short) mentality, and that's not necessarily a bad thing in principle. But those methods often advocate less-than-subtle tactics, such as the *assumptive close,* where you abruptly ask, "What time should I schedule the delivery?" Pushy legacy tactics like these are less than effective in our buyer-empowered market.

Almost always, it's best to get your prospect to close themselves. To do this, make sure that certain conditions are met. The first is value offered. Your prospect should be educated about your offering and the improvement it will bring. This is the tangible outcome that will solve their problems.

The next condition is due diligence. Your prospect may want to compare you to your competition. They may also want a rough idea of the potential returns of an investment in your solution. Help them out. When it comes to competition, we will discuss a tool later that will help guide their comparison (and make you look good in the process).

Finally, they must be prepared and planned. They should have your timelines, step-by-step process descriptions, and other necessary documentation laid out in front of them in a clear and logical manner. Remember to continually qualify your prospect for need, budget, timeframe, and decision-making process so you can help them meet the above conditions.

Overall, what's been the nature of your conversations so far? Sales cycles vary, but you've probably had multiple conversations involving different stakeholders and different concerns. There are lots of moving parts involved. It's likely that, at some point, you stopped being a salesperson and became a consultant. At this point, you will be running out of things to consult about, so the next step will be your prospect's OK to move forward. But with so many elements, including scheduling arrangements and negotiations, it might not be clear when the consulting ends and engagement begins, so make it clear.

Once closing becomes the next logical step, spell out exactly what your prospect needs to do to move forward with you. This will tell them diplomatically, but not too subtly, that it's time to make a decision. For example, you might say something like:

- "To get started, we'll need to get a signoff on our services agreement, and an engagement payment of 50%. But what are the best next steps for you?"

Naturally, from there you will either move forward, or you will discover objections, which you will handle using the strategies we covered earlier.

Action Item #8

In the *Conversation Blueprint*, complete the "Closing" section. Spell out exactly what a prospect would need to do to move forward with you. Ask a good probing question, preferably one that is open-ended, to gauge their reaction about signing on the dotted line.

Following Up and Closing the Sale: Recap

In this chapter, you learned about the middle and end of the sales process. You understand the importance of following up. You can connect the comrades by introducing your prospect to a like-minded colleague. When your prospect goes silent, you can "fall on your sword" and compel a response. You negotiate as a helpful consultant, not a roadblock. Finally, you learned to ditch the antiquated hardsell tactics and get prospects to close themselves through the simple act of defining what "closing" entails.

Next, we'll dive into skills and long-term improvement techniques. You will learn how to practice and edit your script for best results, and there's even a quick health-related sales tip.

4. Staying Sharp

Resource Needed:
- *Conversation Blueprint*

Learning Objective: Improve energy and keep skills sharp
for long-term sales performance.

* * *

In this chapter, we will focus on skills and improvement.
You will learn how to maintain your strengths and push
yourself to new heights. This will involve strategies for
keeping up your confidence and your health.

Using and Revising Your Sales Script

When you first heard the word "script", did you initially
worry that using it would make you sound robotic, or
canned? Hopefully by now you see your script as a
planning tool that will help you keep goals and actions top
of mind.

Your phrasing needs to sound natural, and that comes
from practice. Start by reading your script out loud as you
write it, to make sure it sounds right to you. Once you're
ready, practice a few times with a "ghost prospect" (a voice
in your head). Envision how your typical buyer might
respond to what you say. Next, go through a role-play with
a colleague or friend. Your prospect profiles will help you
and your peer embody the personality. Time yourself, and
stick with typical scenarios.

Once you've written and practiced the script, put it into action. Many of your statements and questions won't be completely new, but your script will build consistency around the things you say. The newer aspects of the script will take getting used to, and may not be perfect right away, so you should consider the first week a testing period. Hone in on what sounds right and what's producing good answers from your prospects.

As a piece of general sales advice, when you face silence after a tough question, let it hang. It might feel uncomfortable, but breathe deeply and relax. Your prospect will fill the air, and often it will be revealing and interesting information. This is an old-school technique used by journalists, and it applies to our world as well.

After your script is ready, you will still need to do some homework before appointments. Thankfully, technology helps immensely in this regard (we'll cover this in the next chapter). When it comes to background information, you should do your research, but don't presume too much about your prospect.

Keep your ears open, and don't be afraid to admit when you don't understand an acronym or some other industry-specific reference from your prospect. I once had a sales appointment with a lady from a compliance firm, and at one point she began to speak heavily in acronyms—for various organizations and federal laws—related to her space. I stopped her and admitted that I was lost. We both laughed, she slowed down, and the rest of the conversation went well. This allowed me to actually understand her buying situation, instead of just pretending I did. The fact is, most of us get caught up in our industry lingo, yet most remember that outsiders don't speak the same language. Your prospect won't think less of you if you ask for clarification; in fact, asking usually has the opposite effect.

When should you review and edit your script? What should you change often, and what should you keep the same? There are no firm rules, but edits make the most sense when it comes time to address new situations that arise more than once. This could be an objection, or an important detail that you had trouble bringing to the surface.

The part of your script that should change more frequently is your pitch. Like a landing page for a product sold online, your pitch is your first big opportunity to sell your offering. You might want to eventually tailor it for each of your prospect profiles. As you test out different aspects of your presentation, gauge your prospect's reaction by asking confirming questions, such as:

- "Does that make sense?"

- "How does that sound to you?"

- "Is that what you had in mind?"

- "Is that clear?"

Make sure that what you say is coming off well. Your prospect might respond dishonestly, so keep an ear out for subtle tonal cues. Test your pitch on multiple prospects so you have a good overall feel for how you resonate.

You need to guide the flow of the conversation, so I recommend that you structure your script similarly to the *Conversation Blueprint*. However, if you do decide to change the structure, make sure you maintain a conversation and not an interrogation.

However, there's one caveat: If your prospect asks for something more than once, give it to them! Don't be afraid to break your structure if your gut tells you it's the right thing to do.

Challenge Yourself

Long-term improvement means avoiding pitfalls, going for ambitious but attainable goals, and making sure you reach new heights in your sales game.

With every call or meeting, challenge yourself in at least one way. Focus on the one thing that scares you most. Many salespeople fear that they will come off as pushy in their persistence to secure a deal or a forward step. Whatever your fear is, focus on it and see how you can improve.

When you get to work, try to get on a sales call within five minutes of arriving. It doesn't matter who you speak with, or the size of the opportunity; the idea is to get up and running right away. This gets you into the right mindset and keeps you there all day. Conversations will only get easier and smoother, and once you get over the initial fear of rejection, it's smooth sailing.

Defeat Self-Doubt

Self-doubt and sales atrophy are huge burdens, but you can overcome them. First, identify the cause by looking at the symptoms. Some doubt is always present when you're facing the possibility of rejection, but here's what to look out for:

Falling back on email — Email is easy, but more often the best approach is to pick up the phone. A real conversation reveals much more than text on a screen. Email won't prevent rejection, if it's coming; at best, it will only delay it. That's not to say that email doesn't ever have an edge over voice, just make sure you're using the former for the right reasons.

Leaving a call with unclear follow-up plans — The prospect says, "Hey, I'll give you a call back next week and let you know what we'll be doing." It's easy to let this fly if you're not vigilant. Always lock it down! you can do this in a natural and un-pushy way by offering something useful in your upcoming follow-up meeting. Just make sure to determine what that thing is before you get to the last lingering moments of the call.

Pushback leading to self-doubt — The prospect dodges or refuses to answer difficult questions, so you back down and throw softballs. At the end of the conversation, you will realize that you don't have enough information to understand and guide the process.

No one likes to be negative, but if something is holding you back, identifying the problem is the first step to fixing it. Be vigilant.

Now that you have identified these obstacles, you are ready to defeat self-doubt, a natural ailment that we all face from time to time. Remember that, when following your script, you will often sound repetitive to yourself, but realize that your words will sound fresh to your prospect. After all, they are hearing you for the very first time!

Keep in mind that you're much more likely to dwell on your failures, the instances when your words *didn't* work for you, than you are your victories. When you win, you probably don't break down what you did right because you are riding high. But when you lose, you pick apart every tiny misstep.

Self-criticism can be valuable if you use it the right way. When you lose a deal, review your process, edit your script and focus on improvement. But don't let self-criticism lead to self-doubt. Remember that losing is part of the game; even the best salespeople in the world might lose around half of their opportunities. Look back to your target close rate and focus on an incremental improvement. Unless your close rate goal is 100% (which is pretty much impossible), failure is built in to the equation; every deal you win comes with a certain number of losses. Or, to put it another way, failure is an investment in future success.

Stand Up

There is one specific, and easy, action you can take to improve both your sales game and your overall health: standing up. Why is this so beneficial? Ultimately, it comes down to increased activity; specifically, if you're standing, you're also more likely to move around.

When you're sitting, your body stops metabolizing, and according to this scary (but factual) infographic, "Sitting is Killing You: The Truth About Sitting Down", sitting for over six hours a day makes you 40% more likely to die within 15 years, compared to someone who sits for three or less hours a day.

You don't have to stand for the entire day. In fact, too much standing has its own negative health effects. But there are significant benefits to spending a large portion of your day on your feet.

If the health advantages aren't convincing enough, you'll be happy to know that standing up can boost your sales game as well. This isn't a profoundly new, revolutionary idea, but it has been proven that your stature and body language affect the way others perceive you, and the way you perceive yourself. A larger, more authoritative stance— or any "stance" at all, compared to sitting—will help you project confidence. This boost will help guide you through tough sales situations.

There's a good reason you don't see the president, rock stars or opera singers sitting when they perform. Standing keeps your diaphragm open, and allows you to project your voice much more effortlessly. If you are accustomed to sitting, it might seem strenuous or even painful to stand for most of the day, but it won't be after you get used to it. It will take about a week to adjust to the change because you'll be using muscles you aren't used to using, but it will be smooth sailing after that.

Also, a corrective mat will make a huge difference; it will take a lot of strain off of your feet and ankles. If it sounds daunting, then start by standing for an hour each day and increase the length of time as you go. Stretching will help too.

There are lots of great, inexpensive options for standing desks and corrective mats. You can check out the standing desk I have used for years, as well as a great mat, on Sales Schema's general resources page.

Earning Quality Referrals

It's no secret that referred leads are much more valuable than other types of leads. Customers are four times more likely to buy when referred by a friend (source: Nielsen). There's no question that referrals are worth their weight in gold, and you should ask for them whenever you can. But when is the right time to ask?

The short answer is this: Ask for referrals whenever your prospect or customer is happy. Some salespeople ask for referrals throughout the entire engagement. But it's not a good habit to oversell; the happiest junctures tend to be when you're hired and when the engagement is successfully executed or completed (either the end of the project, or when the customer expresses satisfaction with your offering).

With that in mind, your customer must have a positive experience for you to expect good referrals. In order to gauge their satisfaction, and also to get valuable feedback, call them up and ask some quick review questions, such as:

- "What was your experience with us like overall?"

- "What did we do right throughout the process?"

- "Where did we fall short?"

- "What could we do better next time?"

Here are a few referral generation tips:

Be upfront — Explain your reason for asking for an intro. Let your prospect or customer know that referrals are an important part of your business.

Be specific — Focus on one particular buyer at a time for your referral campaign. I can't tell you how many partners and networking acquaintances I've been unable to help for the simple reason that they couldn't pinpoint the type of person they wanted to meet.

Help prospect jog ideas — Give them a frame of reference to help them come up with referrals. Suggest a few traits of good referrals, and let them think of people in their world who embody those traits.

Bad referral description: "I want to meet mid-market CEOs who need help with IT."

Good description: "Since we have a track record working with nonprofits, I'd like to meet senior leaders in organizations of 20 or more who have moved offices within the past 3 months, or who have plans to move."

Make it convenient — Offer your referrer an email template to help them make the introduction. Also, limit the size of your ask; start by shooting for just one person.

Here's an example:

```
Hi [Prospect/Customer]

["It was great working with you!" OR "We're all
looking forward to working with you!"].

As you might know, referrals are a big part of
our business, and being a good biz dev person, I
have to ask for them!  Ideal would be [titles,
roles, etc.] in [companies, departments].

Maybe this is someone in another department, a
vendor from a previous project, or maybe an
acquaintance from your office building.  Are
there one or two people you might feel
comfortable introducing?

Best,

[You]
```

If you ask about referrals in a call or meeting, you might get silence in response. If you do, let it hang because it often means they're going through their brain's Rolodex of friends and colleagues.

When you ask for referrals, they might worry that you will force their friends or acquaintances into a pitch, using them, the referrer, as leverage. Always allay this fear. After you make your ask, take the pressure off:

- "Just to let you know, we rarely do business with people right away. Our business usually comes from relationships, and my goal for the meeting with whoever you introduce me to will be strictly informational. I'll learn about their needs, tell them about us, and be on hand if they think we'd be a good fit."

Once you've done that, make it convenient by helping them with the introduction. Offer them an intro template, so all they have to do is copy, paste, and click send. Here's an example:

```
Hi [Referral],

I'd like to introduce you to [You], with whom we
["recently worked"/"will be working"] to do
[whatever it is you do].

I wanted to connect you because you have
complementary experience, and I think you'll have
a great conversation.

I'll let you guys take it from here.

Best,

[Referrer]
```

Action Item #8

In the *Conversation Blueprint*, complete the "Referral Script" section. You can use what we covered and repurpose it, or create something from scratch.

Staying Sharp: Recap

In this chapter, you learned how to start laying the foundation for strong, long-term sales improvement.

You now know how and when to edit, rehearse, practice and test out your script with prospects. Self-criticism is natural, and fear of rejection and other negative impulses must be handled with a positive mindset. Nip self-doubt and sales atrophy in the bud so these forces don't become lingering problems. You now know the health and confidence benefits of standing up. Finally, you became well-versed in the art of securing valuable referrals, which are much more valuable than other leads.

The next chapter will showcase some useful tools to help you in all stages of the sales process. These gadgets will save time and make you more effective.

5. Apps, Tools, and High-Tech Shortcuts

Resource Needed:

- *Competitive Assessment Chart*

Learning Objective: Use technology to win follow-up appointments, take down your competitors, prepare for big meetings, and more.

* * *

This chapter highlights some useful apps, tools, and high-tech shortcuts: web resources, templates, and software you can use to your advantage throughout the sales process. We'll summarize how they work, and where and when they are appropriate.

The first tool is a spreadsheet I made myself, and I've used it for years. It can be used to blow your competition away in one the smartest and most classy ways possible: with data. You can use it to emphasize your strengths and exploit your competitors' comparative weaknesses.

Competitive Assessment Chart

Many companies use some form of the *Competitive Assessment Chart* to make themselves look good when they're stacked against their competition. We will go a step further by providing it to the prospect as a valuable tool, and they can tweak the numbers as they see fit. Here are the steps for guiding your prospect as they fill out the chart:

STEP 1: Review "Considerations" below for insight into what to keep in mind when comparing providers in [your industry].

Ask your prospect to review the considerations for how they will judge you and your competition. The questionnaire at the bottom of the spreadsheet will help drive the comparison. Sell yourself subtly here, by focusing on the areas where you excel and deemphasizing areas where you are weaker. For example, if you're a high-quality provider, focus on what goes into that quality, while taking price out of the conversation. If you are a value provider, focus on value and downplay quality.

Example:

Video Quality Assessment Tool

GOAL: Find the best explainer video studio for your needs.

Directions:

STEP 1: Review "Considerations" below for insight into what to keep in mind when reviewing video quality.

STEP 2: We recommend leaving the existing percentages A8 l8 under "Prioritization" (column C). We think these prioritizations are best, based on our experience creating over 200 videos for over 100 different clients. That said, feel free to alter the percentages based on your priorities, and make sure the total equals 100%.

STEP 3: Input the companies you're comparing under "Co. A" & "Co. B". For our most relevant competitors, go here: www.OURSITE.com/COMPETITORS

STEP 4: Rate each aspect from 1-10 for all companies you're considering (1=worst, 10=best)

Aspect	Prioritization	Co. A (1-10)	Co. B (1-10)	ACME (1-10)
Script	50.00%	7	4	8
Design	20.00%	3	6	9
Animation	15.00%	5	5	10
Sound	10.00%	5	3	7
Experience	5.00%	6	2	6
Overall	100.00%	5.65	4.35	8.3

Here are a few example questions I would use for a video production offering:

- "How well do you understand the product from the video's narrative?"

- "How well do you remember the complex details a few minutes or hours after viewing?"

- "Does the video tell a story?"

STEP 2: We recommend leaving the existing percentages AS IS under "Prioritization" (column C). We think these prioritizations are best, based on our experience. That said, feel free to alter the percentages based on your priorities, and make sure the total equals 100%.

Set up a default set of percentages that emphasize your strengths, but allow them to tweak the numbers freely. This empowers your prospect. Just review the mechanics briefly with them. Make sure to include your company in the first column of the chart.

STEP 3: Input the companies you're comparing under "Co. A" and "Co. B". For our most relevant competitors, go here: [www.OURSITE.com/COMPETITORS]

Instruct your prospect to add a couple of competitors to the chart. You know you are being compared, so you might as well guide the comparison. Referencing relevant competitors will also build trust and confidence.

STEP 4: Rate each aspect from 1-10 for all companies you're considering (1=worst, 10=best).

Finally, have them complete the chart, rating each company on each aspect on a scale of 1 to 10. When they finish, they will have definitive scores for you and your competitors, and you will probably be on top.

When preparing this spreadsheet, pay special attention to the title and goals sections. In the example on the *Competitive Assessment Chart*, I have used the title "Video Quality Assessment Tool". This title is relevant to the example on the chart, and emphasizes "video quality", my example company's differentiator. Your title should match your strongest differentiator. Focus on a desirable business outcome that will grab your prospect's attention.

Lastly, include your logo at the bottom of the sheet. Remember, this is your useful gift to them, so some free advertising never hurts.

Why should you use this chart, and how? First, it will help your prospect make a difficult decision, and your guidance will pull you into their decision-making process. This exercise will build your role as a helpful consultant.

As we covered, the chart accentuates your strengths and downplays your weaknesses. But there are less obvious benefits. For one, it inspires new considerations. I recall many situations where my prospects were completely focused on price. But the interesting pattern I observed is that those same "numbers people" are the ones who most appreciate a comparison tool like this. I offered it to them in a non-pushy way to help them along. I'm not certain they used it much, nor do I think the tool was a major determining factor. What I do know, however, is that they started considering quality aspects that they did not care about earlier. They started asking me questions that had nothing to do with price! Suddenly, they were eager to learn about our process and previous experience. The price sticking point became diluted.

Also, a chart like this will help you stay involved in the decision-making process, even if you aren't allowed to sit in on your prospect's meetings. You offer a schematic, of sorts, to guide them to an informed conclusion.

How and when should you offer this tool? You should think of it instantly if you are told (or start to suspect) that you're going up against competition. Submitting it earlier is always better, as it may help them reach a decision sooner.

The chart also creates a great reason to reconnect, but always make sure to lock down an appointment before you submit it. Here's how you might set it up:

- "By the way, we created a tool for comparing providers. It will let you develop an objective score for each company you're considering. Does that sound like it would be helpful?"

Usually, the prospect will say yes. If they say no, ask them why not. Once they agree, set up an appointment to review it:

- "Great, I'll send it over email. I'd like to learn more about your experience with it and see how I can shed light on the comparison factors. Can we plan on connecting next week? Since I have my calendar in front of me, how about Wednesday at 2 p.m.?"

Timelines

A timeline is a valuable organizational tool, and can be used to help a prospect or customer plan the course of a project from start to finish. However, it can also serve as valuable sales collateral.

As we've discussed, a timeline is a great way to tie your prospect to the calendar, which helps accelerate your sales process in the face of delays and low urgency. A timeline shows when action must be taken in order to enjoy the future value your offering promises.

A great online timeline tool is <u>Tom's Planner</u>. It's fast and clean, and once you make a template it's easy to move things around. They offer a free demo.

In your timeline, focus on three phases: Setup, Implementation, and Wrap-Up. This is the best way to present the process because it clearly separates the steps into a logical beginning, middle, and end. This makes it possible for your prospect to visualize the process, and it gives them a feel for what will be required from them. Once they can visualize it, they will be much more comfortable when it comes time to make the vision a reality.

In the "Setup" phase, make sure your prospect knows what they have to do before getting started. If you need a services agreement, a 50% deposit, or other paperwork, this phase will clarify your onboarding process and create urgency.

The next phase is the engagement itself: the "Implementation" phase. Again, we are helping your prospect get a feel for the experience of working with you.

Finally, the "Wrap-Up" phase includes steps that take place after the solution has been put in place, when the value is realized. This may include a consulting session on how to get the best results from the solution. Also, note an item for receiving final payment and for tying up any other loose ends.

Here are two secrets to help your timeline win you more deals. First, you might wonder what to do if they don't like something in the timeline. What if they are intimidated by all the things happening so fast, or have some other disagreement related to timing? The great thing is, you can collaborate with the prospect to make the timeline fit their needs. In fact, you want this collaboration because your prospect will be investing time and energy, and it's the closest you can get to making the engagement real. The exercise will accelerate your sales cycle and make signing up the next logical step.

The second secret is that you don't have to use the same timeline for everyone. Customize it to meet the challenges and desires of the individual prospect. You might keep the same general structure, but you can add an item or two to cater to their specific pain. For example, if they worry about how their team or superiors will perceive the results of your solution, add a step to the Wrap-Up phase, focusing on the satisfaction of these team members.

Timelines are easy to propose to your prospect; they will almost always be eager to receive them.

You can send the timeline at any juncture after the first meeting. It is best used to hold the prospect to a schedule, when they appear to be delaying or generally lacking urgency. Here's how you might use the timeline to arrange a follow-up appointment:

- "Would it be helpful if I created a timeline to show you what the engagement would look like?"

  (They will most likely answer yes.)

- "Great, I'll send it over in an email. To make sure it's clear and to see if any edits are needed, I'd like to arrange a time to talk briefly next week. Since I have my calendar in front of me, can we aim for Tuesday at 3?"

From there, use the urgency of the timeline dates to maintain communication. After the follow-up meeting, you can say:

- "To make sure we stay ahead of the calendar, I think we should discuss the next best steps on [Date]. Does that work for you?"

A timeline is far more valuable than it first appears. It keeps up urgency, gives you an opportunity to collaborate, and lets you custom-tailor your offering to your prospect's needs in a natural way.

Meeting Preparation With Charlie

Charlie is a GMail app, and it's great for pulling in information about prospects or cold leads before a big call or meeting. It can make research easy and automatic. To use Charlie, first enter your email address. Also, connect your social media accounts so it can pull from your contact list. Once you sign in to the service, you can view Charlie's past briefings, change your settings, or enable or disable networks it pulls data from. You can also change how often it sends you emails.

Charlie will email you before each of your calendar appointments. The message will include a link to a one-page report on the person (or people) with whom you're scheduled to meet, pulled from a variety of sources.

News About Your Prospects with Newsle

Chances are there are things happening right now with your prospects, previous customers and cold leads that might mean new opportunities for you. This may include mergers, acquisitions, or other newsworthy events. If you could stay in the know and reach out to them as soon as these events happen, what would that mean for your business? Newsle is a free and automated tool to keep you informed. It syncs up with your LinkedIn contact list, and it will send you email reports whenever big things happen. The reports contain a wealth of information including press releases, company website updates, articles, and other events.

How should you use Newsle? When major events oocur, be there to congratulate people in your network, or just reach out. Use it to get back in touch with previous customers, or gain insight into new prospects. You can use these events to inform the value offering you extend to them, and fuel the first conversation.

Apps, Tools, and High-Tech Shortcuts: Recap

This chapter showed you some useful tools for all stages of the sales process.

You now know how to use the *Competitive Assessment Chart* as a high-value tool to give you a competitive advantage. With a timeline, you can inspire urgency, cater your offering to your prospect's pain, and give them the experience of working with you. Meeting preparation can be as easy as an automated email, thanks to Charlie. Newsle will tell you about events with your prospects and past customers.

Key Takeaways

Here is a short summary of the material we covered:

Lead Generation — Lead generation is a continuous, daily activity. First, set ambitious but attainable goals. Next, develop and master your lead gen process, then systematize and outsource as much of it as you can.

First Conversation — Keep your first conversation planned, organized and goal-oriented. Your *Conversation Blueprint* will help guide you. Continually qualify your prospects so you understand their buying situation. Finally, transition into a natural and memorable pitch, and always lock down a follow-up appointment.

Follow-Ups and Closing — Get a "yes" during your follow-up conversations by being helpful, building rapport and connecting the comrades. Be "professionally persistent" with unresponsive prospects, and negotiate effectively by maintaining a positive atmosphere. Keep the process moving forward and address concerns until closing is the next logical step.

Skills — Continuously rehearse, edit, and practice your script to ensure long-term improvement. Challenge yourself by getting on a sales call as early in the day as possible. Identify and defeat self-doubt and sales atrophy, and get referrals from your prospects and customers by making the process as easy as possible.

Apps, Tools, and High-Tech Shortcuts — Use technology to help you close deals. Great tools include the *Competitive Assessment Chart*, a timeline (like Tom's Planner) to help your customer visualize the process, the Charlie app to help with pre-meeting research, and Newsle to keep you up-to-date on events among those in your personal network.

I hope you have enjoyed the lessons in this book. If you have completed the Action Items I prescribed, you should be ready to put these ideas to work, and you will be on your way to improving your process and closing more deals.

External Resources

The following is a list of the external resources that I referenced throughout the book.

Note: The items below do not include the custom templates. To access those resources, go here: http://www.salesschema.com/b2b-book-enroll/

Lead Generation Goal Calculator

AeroLeads —

https://aeroleads.com/tools/lead-generation-roi-calculator

Customer Relationship Management Systems (CRMs)

Close.io — http://close.io/

Hubspot Sales Platform—

http://www.hubspot.com/products/sales

PipelineDeals—

http://www.hubspot.com/products/sales

Boolean Search

"Basic Search Tips and Advanced Boolean Explained", University of California, Berkeley — http://www.lib.berkeley.edu/TeachingLib/Guides/Internet/Boolean.pdf

Small Email Research

Rapportive — https://rapportive.com/

Search Modifiers

"Search operators", Google —

https://support.google.com/websearch/answer/2466433?hl=en

"Top 10 Search Modifiers: Why They Matter, What They Are & How To Use Them", SearchEngineLand.com — http://searchengineland.com/top-10-search-modifiers-why-they-matter-what-they-are-how-to-use-them-173343

Press Releases

PR Newswire — http://www.prnewswire.com/

Other Email Research Tools

Email Lookup, Intelius —

https://www.intelius.com/email-search-name.html

Norbert — https://www.voilanorbert.com/

Free Email Verifier — http://verify-email.org/

Cold Email Outreach

"101 Sales Email Templates You Can Use Today to Close More Deals", attach.io — https://attach.io/sales-email-templates/

"Don't Hit Send: 7 Sanity Checks for Sending Cold Email", Lincoln Murphy, *SaaS Growth Strategies* blog — http://sixteenventures.com/cold-email-sanity-checks

Email Tracking Services

Salesforce Tracking — http://www.salesforce.com/sales-cloud/email-tracking-software.jsp

Sidekick by Hubspot — http://www.getsidekick.com/

ToutApp — http://www1.toutapp.com/

Yesware — http://www.yesware.com/

Following Up SlideShare Presentation

"How to Follow Up: Proven Strategies & Email Templates", SlideShare —

http://www.slideshare.net/HubSpot/how-to-follow-up-proven-stratg

Outsourced Work Hiring Services

Fiverr — http://www.fiverr.com

Upwork — http://www.upwork.com

Virtual Staff Finder — http://www.virtualstafffinder.com/

Zirtual — https://www.zirtual.com/

Screen Recording and Video Editing Software

Camtasia — https://www.techsmith.com/camtasia.html

ScreenFlow — http://www.telestream.net/ScreenFlow

Important Sales Stat

"Why 8% of Sales People Get 80% of the Sales", Robert Clay, Marketing Wizdom —

http://marketingwizdom.com/archives/312

Powerful Words

"The Two Most Important Words in Blogging", Brian Clark, Copyblogger —

http://www.copyblogger.com/the-two-most-important-words-in-blogging/

Standing Up Versus Sitting

"Sitting is Killing You: The Truth About Sitting Down", Infographic —

http://www.howtogeek.com/93822/sitting-is-killing-you-infographic/

Standing Desk and Corrective Mat Recommendation

Sales Schema, main resource page —

http://www.salesschema.com/resources/

Referrals

"7 Surprising Stats about Customer Referral Programs", Referral SaaSquatch —

http://www.referralsaasquatch.com/7-surprising-stats-about-customer-referral-programs/

Timeline Tool

Tom's Planner, Online GANTT Charts —

http://www.tomsplanner.com/

Meeting Preparation Tool

Charlie App — https://charlieapp.com/

News About Prospects, Companies, Past Customers

Newsle — https://newsle.com/

Would you do me a solid?

It would be awesome if you would post a short and honest review on Amazon. You'll be helping future readers know what to expect.

Click here and then select the book:

SalesSchema.com/DanAuthorPage

Thanks in advance!

About the Author

Dan Englander is a New York-based author and entrepreneur. As the first employee and Senior Account Manager, Dan helped launch IdeaRocket, the premier studio for high-quality animated explainer videos. He brought in business and managed productions for Fortune 500s and startups like Venmo.

He's the founder of Sales Schema, a site that helps companies win by melding sales and digital marketing. He's the author of *Mastering Account Management* and other business books. In addition, he teaches high-level online courses on B2B sales and marketing.

Previously, Dan was Account Coordinator at DXagency, where he increased digital exposure for clients like Monster Cable and Marc Ecko. He's a decent living room guitarist and he makes a mean paella.

Mortgage: 1170.70
Discover: 250.00
Chase cc: 180.00
US Airways: 131.35
LA Fitness: 29.99
Mountainside: 105.00
Cox: 104.00
SRP: 250.00
water + gas: 150.00
Primerica: 135.00
American Fam: 21.95
Life ins. Yadi
mor Furniture: $100.00
netflix: $ 12.00
Yadi St. loan: $ 430.00
Gas:
Food:
Eating out:
Miscellaneous:

Made in the USA
San Bernardino, CA
28 March 2017